S0-AVH-703

POWER YOUR CAREER:

THE ART OF TACTFUL SELF-PROMOTION AT WORK

RICHARD DODSON & NANCY BURKE

ISBN: 978-1-59298-703-0
Library of Congress Control Number: 2015918877

Printed in the United States of America
Designed by Dan Pitts
First Printing: 2016

20 19 18 17 16   5 4 3 2 1

Beaver's Pond Press, Inc.
7108 Ohms Lane
Edina, MN 55439
(952) 829-8818
www.BeaversPondPress.com

WHAT PEOPLE ARE SAYING...

"In your hands you hold the keys to your future success. Never before has the need for practical and proven-to-work strategies and ideas been greater. If you want to move up in your career or develop your book of business, keep *Power Your Career* within reach and refer to it often. You will be glad you did!"

—MARK LEBLANC
author, *Never Be the Same* and *Growing Your Business!*

"I know that we would see many more people ready for the promotions they are seeking if they read and applied the ideas in this book. Every organization should be teaching these principles and skills to their employees at all levels."

—CHRISTINE WEBSTER MOORE
SVP, chief human resources manager

"Richard Dodson and Nancy Burke have combined forces to write a thoughtful, practical book for managing a career through all the stages of a work life."

—CHRIS FARRELL
author of *Unretirement*

"Knowing, and being able to communicate one's own unique value proposition, is key to moving one's career forward. But how do we do that without turning off the very people we need to influence? How can we do it without being untrue to our own personal style? Richard Dodson and Nancy Burke have created an accessible, practical book that will help readers answer those questions in a way that fits for them. This book is a must for every high school and college career center and every alumni resource office."

—CAROL KAEMMERER
executive branding coach and author of
LinkedIn for the Savvy Executive

"Having coached hundreds of professionals in some facet of career transition, I can say that consistent and effective career management is essential. *Power Your Career* is a comprehensive and effective guide to getting, and staying ahead at work. A must-read!"

—JULIE SCHEIDLER
career coach

"Anyone interested in advancing their career or in being a more engaged person at work would benefit from reading this book! Even if you are not looking to advance greatly in your organization, the tips are fabulous for helping you be a better, more focused, worker."

—CHRISTINE CARNICOM
healthcare brand leader

"*Power Your Career* should be required reading for every college senior or graduate student who wants to 'make it' in the world of work. As a career coach, I can say the skills of tactful self-promotion are essential to virtually every client I have ever worked with."

—MARGIE UNGER DIRKS
CCMC, certified career management coach/trainer

"Unlike many leadership books and seminars, *Power Your Career* provides practical, useful ideas and very specific ways to apply them. I understand networking in a whole new, positive way after reading suggestions on how to connect with other people authentically. If you apply the lessons in this book, you will be a more effective leader and employee."

—SUSAN REINHART
chemist and program manager

"This book was game changing for me, if not life changing. It's practical, inspiring, and energizing. Anyone in any field at any career stage needs this book!"

—ANGELA WEICHMANN
a person who read the book!

CONTENTS

PREFACE

This book didn't start out as a book; it started as conversations with the thousands of people we have worked with in twenty-plus years of career coaching. It grew as we made countless presentations over the last decade on the topic of tactful self-promotion. In that time, we found that many good people were doing good work but not getting ahead. There was a missing ingredient, one that tends to go unspoken: the need to let others know how good you are. Everyone knows it's necessary, but nobody wants to talk about it.

What we share in this book does not come from theory, although we've both read plenty of that. Rather, it comes from our real-world experiences with real people. You'll meet some of them in the pages that follow. As we shared our strategies with more people, we listened as they described their struggles and successes, and we incorporated our learning into our Tactful Self-Promotion framework. We have actually seen people's behavior change over the course of a single networking event following our presentation!

There are many books out there already on the various topics in this book: networking, personal branding, using social media, and more. However, we felt the ideas needed to be pulled into a single framework that addresses how to use all of them together to build your reputation—tactfully.

We hope the ideas in this book will help power your career, as they did for many other people we've worked with. Please visit our website, www.TactfulSelfPromotion.com, for more resources and to share your story with us!

Richard Dodson Nancy Burke

INTRODUCTION

Without promotion, something terrible happens—nothing!

—P. T. Barnum

Imagine you're walking down the hall at work and you run into your boss, who asks a simple question, "How's it going?" This is an opportunity to practice the art of tactful self-promotion. Yet most of us unwittingly pass it up.

Here's a true story that happened to one of us some years ago. Richard and a colleague, Laura, were designing a career transition program. They ran into their boss, Tim, in the hall. When he asked how things were going, Laura responded with enthusiasm, "I'm doing great! I just finished the design for the new Interview Skills seminar I'll pilot on Friday. It's pretty fun, and I think it'll help our clients get jobs faster!" Tim replied, "Sounds great—let me know how it goes!"

Tim then turned to Richard, asking, "And how are you?" Richard looked up and replied with enthusiasm, "Fine." After Tim left, Laura jabbed Richard in the ribs with her elbow and burst out, "What were you thinking? Do you expect him to read your mind? You're doing all this great work—how do you expect him to know what you're doing if you don't tell him?"

And that's the dilemma most of us face. We're doing great work, but we don't know how to make sure those who have influence over our careers see our contribution. Laura wasn't pushy about selling her value, but after that conversation, her boss knew what she was doing and what value she was adding. And what did Tim know of Richard? That he was just fine. At least Richard didn't make things worse, as many do, by complaining: "Everything's fine, if there weren't so much to do . . ." Although this moment was not a setback, Richard didn't use it to enhance his reputation. He missed an opportunity.

Laura's response demonstrates one practice of the art of tactful self-promotion: telling people what you're doing. She doesn't come off as the obnoxious blowhard we associate with shameless self-promotion. You know the type, the ones who constantly blow their own horns and are insufferable at parties. We run from these buffoons! But a *tactful* self-promoter is different. She is confident of and recognized for her achievements and has a good reputation, but isn't constantly telling others how marvelous she is. She finds creative and appropriate ways to further her cause and promote her interests. If she doesn't, who will?

TACTFUL SELF-PROMOTION IS AN ESSENTIAL ART

The art of tactful self-promotion is about cultivating a positive reputation. It isn't about being a blowhard, or always taking the credit, or trying to be the center of attention. It's about becoming visible to the people who can open doors. It's about being seen, ensuring that people know who you are and what an effective resource you are. Tactful self-promotion is an art that, when practiced appropriately and authentically by people who deserve to be recognized, pays off in greater visibility, richer relationships, more interesting assignments, more recognition, and expanded opportunities to use your gifts, make a difference, and secure the rewards you deserve.

Here's the bottom line: in order for you to get ahead, people who have influence and power need to know you exist (do they know your name?), and they need to know what value you might bring to a project or a role (are they aware of your skills and accomplishments?). In short, you need a reputation—a positive one—to showcase the specific skills and qualities you want to be known for.

Tactful self-promotion is an art that, when practiced appropriately and authentically by people who deserve to be recognized, pays off in greater visibility, richer relationships, more interesting assignments, more recognition, and expanded opportunities to use your gifts, make a difference, and secure the rewards you deserve.

Self-promotion isn't optional. The truth is, most of us need to be better self-promoters. In today's world, career management is YOYO (You're On Your Own). You can't expect anyone to take care of you, so you must learn to take care of yourself. Who cares more about your career progress than you do? No one. And if you don't pay attention, your career may stagnate. Your job may even be at risk. No matter how fabulous your performance is, if you don't make your value known to others, then opportunities will pass you by, whereas those who've made sure their worth is recognized will be rewarded with promotions, interesting assignments, enhanced flexibility, and increased protection against layoffs.

WHO NEEDS THIS BOOK?

Tactful self-promotion is an extraordinarily useful and crucial competency throughout your career, whether you're just entering the workforce, starting a new job, building influence in mid-career, conducting a job search, or building a consulting practice or small business.

Early career—If you're just starting your career, you're trying to build a positive reputation and establish yourself at your company. If you don't do this, it's hard to make a difference. It takes influence to get things done, and tactful self-promotion is one tool in your toolkit for exercising influence. You also need it to increase your visibility within your organization and profession to get yourself in the running for emerging opportunities.

Getting started in a new job—Any time you start a new job at a new company, tactful self-promotion is critical for building a positive reputation and getting off to a good start. You need to get your boss on your side, of course, but your peers, your boss's peers, your direct reports, and other influencers in the organization need to hear about you and learn about your capabilities as well.

Building influence in mid-career—One of the most important times to practice tactful self-promotion is when you're already established but feel you've somehow stalled or plateaued. Maybe you made a splash a couple of years ago, but since then you've just been working away—making a difference but not necessarily getting the attention you once did. The danger here is that your colleagues may think they know what you can do, but they may not know your goals or what you've been learning or doing more recently. It's time to get noticed again.

Initiating a career change—Similar to those who need a mid-career boost, those who want to shift to a different profession, move from a technical position into management, or move from one organization to another must build visibility for skills they may not be using in their current positions. The challenge is to be known for the skills and competencies required in the new role, profession, or industry—that is, to build a reputation for something new. This can be done, and it can be fun, but it takes a deliberate strategy.

Conducting a job search—Most people face a career stage when they are between jobs and conducting a job search. During such transitions, it's critical to build visibility with people of influence in your profession. Many of the strategies we'll recommend will be useful for job seekers or can be easily adapted to work at this stage.

Freelancing, consulting, or entrepreneurship—Entrepreneurs—especially freelancers, solo practitioners, and consultants—build their businesses through referrals. Their careers are driven by a specific, positive reputation, and the art of tactful self-promotion is crucial to their success.

No matter what your particular career situation, the art of tactful self-promotion will help you get where you want to go.

THE CORE STRATEGIES OF TACTFUL SELF-PROMOTION

Tactful self-promotion isn't a single skill. It is a set of practices that creates a rich foundation on which to build career success. We focus on three big ideas in this book: Positioning Yourself, Cultivating Strategic Relationships, and Increasing Your Visibility.

THE ART OF TACTFUL SELF-PROMOTION AT WORK

POSITION YOURSELF →

- Be Worthy
- Craft Your Brand and Value Proposition
- Share Accomplishments and Learnings
- Project a Powerful Presence

CULTIVATE STRATEGIC RELATIONSHIPS →

- Get Your Mindset Right - It's about Relationships
- Develop Your Networking Strategy
- Expand Key Relationships
- Maximize Executive Contacts

INCREASE YOUR VISIBILITY

- Make Meetings Matter and Learn to "Work a Room"
- Promote Your Team and Your Department
- Leverage LinkedIn and Social Media
- Be Seen as a Thought Leader

Each core strategy encompasses many possible actions, and we'll discuss many of them. But don't worry—you don't need to do everything we outline all at once. You need only to pick one place to start. But in order to figure out your best approach, it helps to have the big picture in mind.

1. *Position Yourself*

In order to have something worth promoting, you need to be doing a terrific job and adding value to your organization. In other words, "Be worthy." You need to know how you want to be seen—your reputation and your brand—and then you need to develop a value proposition that is easy to share, one that people will remember and pass on to others. You also need to become comfortable sharing what you're working on, what difference you're making, and what you're learning that is relevant to your profession. Finally, you need to make sure that the "package" people see represents the content inside. In other words, you need to project a professional image and presence through your appearance and demeanor.

2. *Cultivate Strategic Relationships*

No matter how compelling your value proposition, your career will not take off if you don't have people on your side to help power it. Cultivating authentic, lasting relationships is key to career success. It's the heart of tactful self-promotion. As with positioning yourself, cultivating relationships requires a goal: Why do you want to broaden and deepen your professional relationships? And whom do you want to include in your circles of relationships? Once that's clear, you can create a strategy for initiating new relationships, building allies, and cultivating advocates, giving special attention to your boss and other executives in your organization and industry.

3. Increase Your Visibility

Once you are comfortable talking about your value and have ignited your network, look for additional ways to elevate your visibility. The goal of these strategies is to cultivate a reputation with people you don't yet know. If you're a manager, you can also apply the art of tactful self-promotion to your department. You can expand visibility and your network by attending networking events, using LinkedIn and other social media sites wisely, publishing articles or blog posts, speaking in public, or even appearing in the media. Don't be scared away! There are many ways to cultivate a reputation as a thought leader, and we guarantee you will be able to implement these strategies if they are appropriate for your goals.

Many people believe they face unique challenges in the self-promotion arena, and they are probably right. Introverts, people from cultures in which self-promotion is taboo, and women in traditionally male fields are just three examples of people with special challenges. While we agree that some people face greater obstacles to self-promotion than others, we believe anyone who wants better professional visibility will find useful ideas and tips in this book. We haven't dedicated separate sections to these common issues; rather, we have integrated ideas that can be adapted to specific situations.

UNDERLYING PRINCIPLES

By its nature, self-promotion can be misunderstood as being self-centered or selfish. But in fact, if done well, self-promotion builds stronger relationships. What comes to mind when you hear the words *self-promotion*? For most of us, it isn't a positive image. When we ask audiences this question, the words that generally pop out are *bragging*, *selfish*, *obnoxious*, and *inauthentic*. Self-promotion doesn't have to be any of these things, yet when we add *tactful* to the phrase, people look at us with suspicion. Like oil and water, tact and self-promotion don't seem to mix. But in fact, like oil and vinegar, these elements can come together to create an essential and welcome combination that spices up your career prospects.

Here are a handful of principles that are important when thinking about self-promotion. They underscore all the strategies we lay out.

Be Worthy

If you don't have substance—if you've not been doing top-notch work—then don't start focusing on self-promotion yet. If you're not a strong performer or a team player, then even *tactful* self-promotion will backfire. We know of one man, highlighted in the *Minneapolis Star Tribune* who successfully climbed from an entry-level role to become a senior leader at Target, and he recalled that his sole focus was to be the best at his job: "Ultimately, my advice is this: regardless of how important or basic your role is, be accountable for your performance and take advantage of opportunities to build meaningful connections. Treat others as you would want to be treated. Be the best in something and below average in nothing." We believe this is very sound advice.

Be a Giver

Relationships are the heart of success, in life as well as in business. Promoting yourself does not have to come at the expense of others.

In fact, the best way to build a positive reputation is to genuinely care about others, uncover their needs and concerns, and find ways to give back. For many of our clients, including those who really resisted reaching out beyond their comfort zones, the relationships they built became their biggest reward—bigger than the doors opened or opportunities uncovered. You'll see a bias in this book toward giving, not because it's a great strategy for getting (although things do tend to come back to you), but because it's a better way to live and it leads to greater happiness and success.

Be Prepared

Successfully establishing these new behaviors is not about implementing a big system or completing a complex set of steps. It's more about forming habits and being prepared to leverage opportunities that arise in your life. We've found that a few new habits (or even just one new behavior), implemented consistently over time, can have a big payoff. Your task is to first become more aware of what you already do to shape your reputation (good and bad) and then to stop doing things that are not helping you and start doing things that will. You don't usually plan for opportunities to promote yourself; rather, they're serendipitous happenings. You run into the CEO or an industry expert in a hallway, or you are asked to speak up unexpectedly. Being prepared means practicing the behavior you want to demonstrate at these times. If you don't practice these behaviors, you won't be ready when opportunity strikes. We'll help you build habits and prepare to use the moments that emerge, and you'll be on your way to career success.

Be Authentic

Dictionary definitions of *authentic* include "genuine, real," "true to one's own personality, spirit, or character," and "not false or copied." We want you to be yourself—but to be your *best* self! Some of the models and strategies we teach may be second nature to you and easy to implement. Others may push you beyond your comfort zone. And still others may be things you'll simply never do. An introvert, for example, is not likely to become the life of a party. However, introverts *can* prepare a few questions ahead of time to make conversations more fruitful when they mingle.

We're not suggesting a personality overhaul; rather, it's a matter of applying these tools and finding ways to use them that feel sincere. That is what makes self-promotion both tactful and an art. As you explore these ideas in more detail, we'll challenge you to try out different tools. At first, you probably won't feel authentic. But after you practice using them and tweaking them to your circumstances and personality, you'll find your authentic style. Use this guide not as prescription but as inspiration for developing your own personal approach to tactful self-promotion.

LET'S GET STARTED!

Throughout the book we'll provide practical approaches to building your self-promotion campaign, and these approaches are buttressed with numerous real-world examples pulled from our own lives as well as the lives of those with whom we've worked. As you read, try to identify a handful of things that appeal to you and that you would feel comfortable trying out. You don't have to change everything you are doing. A shift here, a new idea there, and you'll be on your way to not just earning but actually *getting* the visibility, opportunities, and recognition you deserve!

SECTION ONE

POSITION YOURSELF

POSITION YOURSELF

What makes you unique, makes you successful.

—William Arruda

Fact: you have a reputation. When you leave the room and people talk about you, do you know what they say? Are they conveying a message that moves you toward your goals? It is your job to know how you want to be seen and then to take action to be seen in that particular way. That is the essence of tactful self-promotion. How you position yourself matters. Just doing good work isn't enough. You need a clear and compelling response to the question "What do you do?" or "What differentiates you?" or "What kind of work are you looking for?" You have a great deal of influence over how you're seen. But it takes some thought and some work to clarify your personal brand.

We'd like to introduce you to four worthy individuals whose careers are at different stages. They all are struggling to be seen in a way that opens the opportunities they want. They feel somehow out of their depth when it comes to a moment critical to their next career step. Read their stories and see if you have you ever found yourself with a similar challenge.

NATASHA, a director of marketing at a large consumer packaged-goods company, has ambitions to move up into senior management. But she's been in this role for nearly five years and hasn't reached the executive ranks. She is trying to broaden her marketability and would love to get some international experience. So she is excited when she gets wind of a new task force focused on expanding a product line into Latin America. She wants to be on that team! It just so happens that the executive sponsor of the task force is coming to town. When Natasha has a chance to introduce herself, she states with enthusiasm, "I'm a director of marketing. I've been in this position for five years, and I love it—it's been a great learning experience!" In retrospect, she's not sure she made quite the impression she had hoped.

GEORGE is an independent consultant focused on finance. He is a CPA and does some investment work. He's not only very knowledgeable but also trusted by the people who know him. He had a great reputation in his role at Tricom Limited, where colleagues and internal clients often praised his work and said things such as, "You should go out on your own." A year ago he finally decided to take the plunge and start a consulting practice. When he shared his plan with his connections, they responded with enthusiasm. One longtime advocate offered to help, saying, "I'm happy to introduce you to some folks. Tell me who your ideal customer is and what makes you and your services different from your competitors'." There was a long pause. George was stumped.

MEI recently graduated with a degree in human resource management. She worked her way through college as a waitperson, and she continues to wait tables on the weekends. Weekdays, she's been taking on some temporary assignments as an administrative assistant. She recently secured an interview for an HR specialist position with a large company in town. It's a job she really wants, and her college degree has prepared her well. To open the interview, the hiring manager gave her a chance to set the stage by stating, "Tell me about yourself." Mei started out, "I'm currently a waitperson at the Lexington Grill. I've worked there for over four years." As she watched the interviewer's face, Mei couldn't help but feel she was somehow missing the mark.

HENRY is an IT professional recently laid off from a large software development company. He had been an outstanding employee, but his company restructured, eliminating his job along with thousands of others. He needs to find work, but he's not sure he wants to go back into a corporate culture. He decides to call a friend who recently landed a new job. His friend greets him with warmth, commiserates for a moment, and then asks Henry, "What type of role are you looking for?" Henry replies, "Well, I'm very flexible. I'll take just about anything, really. Hey, your company is really close to my house—do you know if there are any openings?" Unfortunately, this response was not his best move.

These situations are far too common. Natasha, George, Mei, and Henry are all good, talented performers. But in these scenarios, they fell short of what they wanted to accomplish. They didn't move their careers forward.

Knowing and articulating your value is a critical career skill. But don't make the mistake of thinking that self-promotion is all about you. Although you need to be prepared with a compelling message, cultivating a great reputation isn't as much about tooting your own horn as it is about paying attention to others and acting in a way that makes you worthy of a great reputation.

This is the first step, and thankfully our four new friends are in good shape. They are competent, reliable workers. They just don't know how to elevate their visibility. In this first section, we'll walk you through starting your promotion campaign on a firm foundation as someone genuinely worthy of promotion. Then we'll explore how to define your value and communicate that value to others—with your words as well as your demeanor.

POSITION YOURSELF

- Be Worthy
- Craft Your Brand and Value Proposition
- Share Accomplishments and Learnings
- Project a Powerful Presence

Here's what to expect in this section:

Chapter 1: Be Worthy

In order to promote yourself, you need to offer something worth promoting. You need to be doing a terrific job and delivering results for your company. You need to be constantly learning about your job, organization, profession, and industry. And you need to be someone others want to work with. We'll outline the behaviors worth cultivating that will ensure your self-promotion campaign is built on a solid foundation of your genuine worth.

Chapter 2: Craft Your Brand and Value Proposition

You already have a personal brand—it's your reputation. In order to really build a brand, you need to answer the question, "What do you want to be known for?" Then you need to craft a unique value proposition—a statement that is easy to communicate and that will be remembered and shared by those who hear it. If you can't articulate your value, how can you expect others to do so? We'll give you a structure for organizing this content and plenty of examples of what a great value proposition sounds like.

Chapter 3: Share Accomplishment and Learnings

You may be uncomfortable talking about your accomplishments. But sharing what you're working on, what difference you're making, and what you're learning is an important skill. Your boss and other people of influence need to hear about the work you are doing. But they don't necessarily need to hear it directly from you—it's even more powerful when they hear it from your customers and colleagues. You can have a hand in making this happen. We'll show you how.

Chapter 4: Project a Powerful Presence

Presence and image are about as hard to explain as charisma and charm, but you know who has it and who doesn't. You project a presence and an image through your body language, demeanor, and dress. What messages do your posture, clothes, and hairstyle send? And as cliché as it sounds, your handshake really does matter. The way you present yourself influences how others see you, what gets said about you, and ultimately what opportunities come your way. This chapter will help you align your personal presence with your goals.

If you work through these four ideas seriously, you'll be well on your way to building a reputation that will unlock the opportunities you're seeking.

CHAPTER 1

BE WORTHY

You can't build a reputation on what you're going to do.

– Henry Ford

The Wizard of Oz was a powerful self-promoter, and it worked for a while. But he was eventually found out as a charlatan, with his public image truly made of smoke and mirrors. If tactful self-promotion is to be truly tactful and have lasting results, then you have to be promoting the real thing!

If tactful self-promotion is to be truly tactful and have lasting results, then you have to be promoting the real thing!

Have you ever worked with someone with a reputation for being an empty suit? We have. She put on a good show. She dressed well and spoke well, and her office was full of fancy furniture. Her credentials were mounted on the wall in impressive frames. But when carefully viewed, the "credentials" turned out to be only a country club membership and an award for supporting a local charity. And when it came to delivering results, she dropped the ball. Nobody could point to anything she had accomplished. In fact, when she did get a plum assignment, she nearly tanked the project. When we peeked behind the curtain, there wasn't much there. The discrepancy between her image and the reality of what she delivered eventually became clear, and her opportunities dried up. She simply wasn't worthy of promotion. She would have done well to focus first on delivering real value and then on her image.

When you are worthy of promotion, then you'll begin to build a positive reputation simply because you deserve it. Then you'll be in a terrific position to start increasing your visibility, and cultivating a reputation within an ever-growing community. Here are a few ideas to help you build a solid foundation for your career.

ALWAYS PERFORM AT YOUR BEST!

Reputation is based in large part on how well you perform the work you've been assigned. Even if it's a job you don't want, such as Mei's job as a waitperson, you must deliver the best value you can if you want to build an authentic reputation as someone who delivers on what you promise.

Do Your Job Really Well

In fact, do it better than it's ever been done before! There is no substitute for doing excellent work. We all know employees who coast through their jobs, doing just what's necessary. Have you ever heard a colleague say, "That's not in my job description"? That might be true, but doing just what's in your job description rarely gets you noticed or promoted. No matter what type of job you have, going above and beyond what is expected can make you stand out.

Although Mei's service job isn't what she wants to do long term, she does understand the importance of doing it well in order to build a positive reputation and secure a solid recommendation, not to mention to make it a point of personal pride.

For starters, Mei offered to take unpopular shifts. She stayed and covered when others didn't show up. She listened to customers and made some menu suggestions she believed would be popular. Because she was such a good employee and had good relationships with her shift supervisors and the restaurant manager, her ideas were heard and some of them moved forward. In fact, when the corporate group asked for input from the field, Mei was invited to attend the brainstorming session, making her more visible within the organization—including with the HR reps.

There is a lot of talk these days about employee engagement, and Mei has chosen to be a very engaged employee. Studies involving thousands of employees in many different fields have shown that employees such as Mei, who feel connected to and interested in their work, enhance not only their reputations but also their employers' bottom lines. More than ever, corporations and managers are aware of the importance of an engaged workforce. This provides opportunities for the really engaged employee to get noticed and, importantly, to get recognized for the value she is delivering.

In order to become valued by your organization, you have go beyond the basic requirements and add value every quarter, every month, every day. But good work alone is not necessarily enough. You have to find ways to do the job better than others have, setting the bar higher and creating the new standard for how the job should be done. Increase efficiency, improve quality, and always deliver more than you promise.

Offer Solutions Instead of Complaints

Most workplaces are full of problems and full of complainers. Differentiate yourself by making suggestions for how to resolve problems. Genuinely try to be part of the solution. Look for ways to do things more quickly or accurately; search for solutions to the problems that frustrate your team. Start a habit of asking yourself, "Is there a better way?"

As you identify a way to make things better, take it to the next step: create a process, procedure, template, worksheet, or tool—whatever will help others implement this improvement. Then let people know you may have an easier way to do something and offer to share your approach. Don't push it on others. Don't brag at a meeting. Just offer that you have ideas for improvements should others have an interest. Then let them come to you. In the meantime, use your improvements to do a better, more efficient job yourself.

No organization is perfect, and there are always problems to be solved, so each of us is constantly given the opportunity to choose how we want to respond. People have two common responses when faced with a problem. They can adopt what neuroscience calls a "fixed mindset," throwing their hands up in resignation and continuing to do the same thing they had been doing, instead of initiating change. Alternatively, they can adopt a "growth mindset," believing there are better ways to do things and actively seeking out solutions. The growth mindset is the cornerstone of resilience, a defining characteristic of the engaged employee and certainly one of the biggest keys to success in any endeavor. When things go south, people typically get stressed and defensive, a brain state that is not conducive to solving problems. The standout is the person who can stay focused on the right question—"What are we going to do about this?"—rather than the wrong one—"How the heck did this happen?"

We each have the capacity to adopt a growth mindset and even to transform from a complainer to a solution provider. The effort of making the change is so worthwhile—it really is more fun to solve problems than to complain about them, and it's good for your career. So what can you do today to make your workplace a bit better?

BE A STUDENT OF THE GAME

Before you start promoting yourself, you need to be in the game: engaged in your profession and organization. You are one of many players competing to reach long- and short-term goals. To get ahead, you need to know more than the basic rules. You need to strategize. Your career takes place in a larger world, and if you're not in tune with that world, it's hard to make good decisions about whom to connect with, what information to share, and what you need to be learning to stay relevant. It's *your* job to do this—you can't count on your company to steer you in the right direction. You're in charge, so you need to decide to be in the game.

Stay Fresh and Current

Doing your job is important, but you also need to build skills that will be needed in the future, even if your company isn't telling you to do so. Stay current on emerging technologies as well as best practices for your profession. Get active in professional associations, read professional journals, follow an intriguing blog or two, and participate in a couple of LinkedIn groups focused on your area of expertise.

Richard learned this lesson decades ago, when he was a young career coach in Silicon Valley. He was working with a big microchip manufacturer that was planning some layoffs. During a tour of the plant, he was escorted into a giant room (he claims it was the size of a football field). It was full of drafters. Yes, drafting tables and pencil sharpeners and pads of paper. Row after row of desks. Now, these were fantastic employees, the best of the best, manually drafting multilevel circuit boards and other complex components. They were loyal, long-term resources, wonderful team players who never missed a day of work and took every course the company asked them to take. You get the idea. Richard turned to the HR representative and asked, "Do they all know they'll be laid off?" She told him they weren't on the list.

But even Richard knew that AutoCAD was on the way in, and manual drafting would soon be a thing of the past. Not that month, but not long after, a new CEO was named, and soon that whole group learned their jobs were being eliminated. Some of the drafters were shocked, but they shouldn't have been. They hadn't looked up from their desks long enough to see where their profession was going. Others had been paying attention. They had been taking classes at night, on their own time, to stay current in their field. And each of those drafters raised a hand and said, "I know AutoCAD. And I can train others!" These folks kept their jobs and became leaders in their field.

It really is easy to get focused on a job and forget to look at larger trends and the skills they'll demand in the future. But you've got to do it, or you're vulnerable. Do you know what trends are affecting your company, your industry, and your profession? If not, it's time to start scanning the horizon.

STAYING ON TOP OF TRENDS

Here are a few ideas for staying in touch with important trends.

- Join a LinkedIn group. Pay attention to the conversation. What questions are people asking? What are people concerned about?
- Subscribe to an online journal in your field.
- Join a professional association and read their materials (from both the local and the national chapters).
- Follow your industry's thought leaders online. What are they writing about on their blogs and in social media? Follow them on Twitter to see what they are posting.
- Set up Google Alerts to send you notices when things related to a specific trend appear in the news.

If you put just two hours a month into tracking trends, you'll be far ahead of others. Even better, you'll also be expanding your network, which we'll talk more about in section 2.

When Henry, the IT guy looking for work, starts seriously reviewing job postings, he keeps running into requirements related to Cloud technology. This is clearly a hot skill. Henry needs to gain some knowledge about this important area, so he takes action to get up to speed. He starts by interviewing a couple of his colleagues who specialize in this area to discuss where things are going and what specific skill sets they recommend if he wants to remain competitive. They are happy to share their perspectives. He gets interested and takes a class at the local community college, and he also checks out some blogs to see who's on the cutting edge. He can now talk with enthusiasm about Cloud technology, even if he doesn't have a lot of experience with it. His knowledge of what is going on in his industry and his willingness to pursue new skills will impress hiring managers.

Connect Your Learning to Your Company's Needs

Success at a company is not just about staying current in your profession and industry—it's also about applying that knowledge to help your organization accomplish its goals. What trends do you see? What are the implications for your company? Your department? What does that tell you about where you might add the greatest value? The key here is to think about how you can connect the emerging trends in your profession to the challenges your company or industry is facing. This adds value. And it gives you something real to promote.

Staying on top of trends is one of Natasha's strengths. In fact, after attending a national conference, where she heard about emerging ideas on digital marketing, she spearheaded the first digital campaign at her company. Unfortunately, she was quiet about it. But she's well positioned to start promoting herself and these valuable skills.

BE SOMEONE PEOPLE WANT TO WORK WITH

In today's world of work, being an effective member of a team is critical to both your ability to get things done and your efforts to build your reputation. A great team member is invested in the results of the team as a whole and interested in the success of each team member. Adopt this attitude, do your part, help out when you can, and you'll be the kind of team member others want to work with. As your reputation for making a contribution grows, you'll be more likely to be invited to participate on task forces and special project teams. It pays to play well in the sandbox. Increasingly, workplaces accept that a great team will more often than not beat a loose collection of talented individuals. This is a skill set well worth developing.

Bring Joy to Your Work

It's not just what you do that makes you valuable at work; it's who you are! The enthusiasm and vitality you bring to work raise everyone's level of energy and motivation. So maintain a positive attitude—be the person who makes others happy to pitch in.

Have you ever seen an executive come through your office and leave the place a little more optimistic and upbeat than it had been? Just interacting with him or her makes you feel like an important member of the team. Have you also encountered the other type of executive, the one who seems to have no interest in the people in that office, who is just there to meet with a customer or division head? Everyone feels relieved when this executive finally leaves. But executives who bring enthusiasm and an interest in others every time they enter a room grow their reputations and secure loyalty and engagement from their employees.

You don't have to be an executive to influence the mood and culture of an organization. Can you think of someone—not an executive but perhaps an admin or a techie—who brightens the mood just by coming through the office? It's not what these people do but rather who they are that makes them influential. Similarly, your attitude can be a significant career asset—or a derailer.

Keep Your Word

Act with honor and keep your word. People need to learn to rely on you, and they can do this only if you consistently do what you say you will do. If you promise a report by 3:00 p.m., get it in by 3:00. If you know you'll miss a deadline, alert those involved as soon as you figure it out, not at the last minute. Let them know the reason for the delay and the new delivery time. Show that you care about following through on your promises. This habit alone will take you a very long way toward cultivating a positive reputation.

Ask What You Can Do to Help

When a colleague is overwhelmed, offering to take over even a menial task will brighten her day. Bonding with your colleagues often happens during the roughest periods of work. If you see those periods as opportunities to be of use to your colleagues, you will reap the benefits. Sharing knowledge, training, and tricks you've learned can also be helpful: "I've set up a macro to make that faster. Would you like a copy?" or "I took a course on this. Would you like to borrow the reference sheet?"

Of course, you have to deliver what you promise without overcommitting yourself, but a little time assisting your colleagues goes a long way toward a positive reputation. Stepping in and offering your help builds goodwill. And when you really need the help, people will be there. (We'll talk more about promoting your department and colleagues, in addition to yourself, in chapter 10.)

George built a great deal of his reputation by helping others in his department and elsewhere in the company. He was generous with his time, coaching younger employees on technical accounting questions, as well as management and career skills. On task forces he often volunteered to write and present the group's reports. In these ways, George built capital for his career that he was able to leverage when he decided to launch his own business.

Share the Credit

Self-promotion doesn't mean you're always talking about yourself. In fact, talking about the accomplishments of others is a great way to be recognized as a gracious supporter of others. There's that team concept again. You can't lose! Let others know you appreciate their contributions, and make the effort in meetings to acknowledge the specific contributions of others. Bragging about others can be good for your career.

In contrast, there's a downside to not sharing the credit. One of our clients, Julie, was shocked when her colleague Reginald mentioned in a meeting that "he" had just secured a new contract—one that Julie had an equal role in securing. This led to some short-term visibility for Reginald. But in the long term, it caused him trouble. In fact, had Reginald given some credit to Julie, he still would have gotten attention: he would have been seen as someone who gets things done, but he also would have been cast in a more generous light. Sharing the credit is not only the right thing to do; it's a much better strategy for building the reputation and relationships that move a career forward. One of the complaints about shameless self-promoters is that they hog all the credit. If you get in the habit of sharing the credit, you'll never be accused of being such a pig!

> *Bragging about others can be good for your career.*

IF YOU ARE WORTHY, YOU ARE READY!

A positive and lasting reputation must be built on a foundation of solid work, engaged learning, and caring about those you work with. If you start to promote yourself before you've proven to yourself and others that you are worthy, all your self-promotion efforts could collapse. You'll just look like one of those blowhards or empty suits none of us can stand. But if you are a quality person building on a foundation of delivering quality work, then you are ready to start the process of actively promoting yourself—tactfully!

BOOSTING WORTHINESS

If you take an honest look at your current situation and suspect that you're underperforming, how can you step it up?

- Reflect on what might be contributing to your underperformance. Is it lack of skills, lack of interest, the environment, or something else? Make a list of ways you might address those problems, which might include taking a class, requesting to cross-train in other departments, making a job change, or even something as simple as deep cleaning your office.
- Talk with a few people you think are outstanding performers and find out what motivates their strong performance.
- Set up a conversation with your supervisor and ask for candid feedback. Listen carefully to that feedback and create a plan to respond to it—positively!

TAKE ACTION TO POWER YOUR CAREER

If you think you need to work on being worthy, take a few minutes and consider the following actions:

- Think of three things you already do that make you confident you are worthy of self-promotion.
- Identify two areas to focus on that would make you a better, more pleasant, more productive team member and improve your worth.
- Stay current on trends in your profession—set up Google Alerts, follow some thought leaders on Twitter, participate in a professional association. Then apply those learnings to make a difference on the job.

Start today.

CHAPTER 2

CRAFT YOUR BRAND AND VALUE PROPOSITION

All my life I've wanted to be someone;
I guess I should have been more specific.

–Jane Wagner / Lily Tomlin

Whether you like the idea of personal branding, you already have a brand—it's your reputation. You might not know what it is, and it might not be the one you want. Most likely, you aren't taking action to shape your reputation.

So let us ask you this: "Does Pope Francis have a personal brand?" Well, of course he does. What does he stand for? Can you give examples of how he lives out certain values or beliefs? How does what he stands for compare with that of the previous pope (Benedict) or the one before him (John Paul II)? Each pope has projected a very different brand. It isn't that the papacy in general has a brand (although it does provide a foundation against which each individual defines himself). What shapes each brand is the personality, the values, the particular actions each individual models.

Pope Francis was clear from the moment he took his new office what kind of image (and substance) he wanted to cultivate—from the shoes he wore to the transportation he chose, from his housing to every address he delivered. Most of us have not met the pope and don't know what he's like as an individual, but what he stands for is pretty clear from his actions and words—his brand is distinct. Most people have to work harder than the pope to get attention, but the principle of knowing what you stand for and how to articulate those ideas in your life is the same.

IDENTIFY YOUR BRAND

Remember George, the finance professional starting a consulting practice? Well, he's experiencing some difficulties. The people he talks to about his practice are friendly, and they tell him how much they believe in him, but he isn't getting any business or referrals. He can't quite figure it out, until he meets with an old friend, Lee, who is really well connected. After George explains what a good finance person he is, Lee replies, "George, I won't refer you to my network"—George's heart skips a beat, but Lee continues—"*until* you are clear about where you can add the greatest value."

George hadn't approached his marketing this way. He didn't want to narrow his options, so he had been emphasizing the breadth of his capabilities rather than focusing on specific areas of expertise. He thought that to get business, he should be open to everything. But positioning himself as a great all-around finance guy just wasn't getting him traction.

So he takes Lee's message to heart and looks closely at his skills and interests to discern the work he really wants to do and the problems he really wants to solve. Where can he make the biggest difference? What type of work is best suited to him? With whom does he want to work? Only he can answer those questions, so he makes time to really think about it and try to discover the answers.

Now it's your turn.

Get to Know Yourself

The process of defining your brand requires a bit of soul searching, but it's worth the effort. It takes focus to really explore these big questions: What matters to you? What are you great at? What motivates you? George put together a list of questions he thought he needed to answer in order to move forward with confidence. You may want to ask them of yourself too.

- What kinds of work do I look forward to doing?
- What kinds of work do I perform particularly well?
- What kinds of problems do I really like to solve?
- Where can I make the biggest difference?
- With whom do I want to work?
- What makes me unique?
- If I were competing with two hundred other people for a job, what would differentiate me? Why would someone want to talk with me?

It can also be very helpful to get some outside perspective, so do some research on yourself. Here are a few ideas:

- Take a look at your old performance reviews. This not only helps you remember some of your accomplishments and get a better handle on your strengths, but it can also give you specific words and phrases to use in describing your brand or professional image.
- Take a personal assessment test online or with the assistance of a coach. For example, StrengthsFinder 2.0 can help you identify strengths, and it gives you a robust report with lots of words to work with when trying to articulate what you are good at.

- Visit the bookstore or library and page through some of the many good books on career assessment, decision making, career change, finding your purpose, and other career topics. Choose one or two that seem to fit you best and do any exercises they recommend.
- If you are at a crossroads and really need to make some significant decisions, or if you are unclear about your career direction, then it would be worth seeking out a career coach to partner with you. A coach will ask you the tough questions that are sometimes hard to ask yourself, help you with assessments, give you feedback on your career, and make suggestions for you to consider.

Check out the resources page on our website, www.TactfulSelfPromotion.com, for more recommendations.

Find Out How Others See You

Once you take stock of yourself, it's important to get another point of view, that of your friends, colleagues, and other people who know you well. They may tell you about things they admire that you take for granted as just part of who you are; these qualities are important because they might be things that differentiate you from others. Other people might also help you see some ways to improve yourself and your reputation.

Seeking feedback from others also gives you information that can shape your self-promotion plan. If people already see you as having strengths that support your objectives, then your job is to reinforce that idea. But if people don't see you as having the skills or qualities required to support the next step you'd like to take in your career, then you need to develop a plan to make those skills and qualities visible. So, just how do you find out how others see you? Here are some ideas.

If you've been in a leadership role in a large company, you've probably already taken what's called a "360° Assessment." The idea is to collect data about yourself from all around—from your boss, peers, direct reports, and possibly vendors or customers with whom you work closely. Learning how these different stakeholders view you can be invaluable. If you've done this before, pull out your results and take a look—with an open mind—to see where you stand. If you haven't, or if your last assessment was a while ago, read on.

By far the best way to find out how others view you is to ask them. Whom can you ask? Bosses, former bosses, colleagues, customers, direct reports, and anyone else who has held a stake in your career at some point. These are the people who help shape your reputation. So, how do you open these conversations? Follow one of our rules of thumb: be honest and simply tell them why you want their frank input. If you just ask people out of the blue, "What do you think about me?" you'll likely get fairly cautious responses. You'll get more open responses if you explain that you're taking a personal inventory and doing some career planning, and that you would really benefit from their input.

By far the best way to find out how others view you is to ask them.

Ask questions about what they see as your strengths and your weaknesses. Ask what they see as your next career step. And finally, ask what behaviors you should continue that support your reputation and what you might want to change in order to enhance your reputation. Here are some sample questions to consider asking when seeking feedback about your reputation.

- What are three or four words you might use to describe me?
- From what you've seen while working with me, what would you say are my strengths, outside of any particular technical skills?
- If you were coaching me, what would you advise me to change in order to improve my performance or reputation?

Stay open to people's feedback. Once you ask for it, it's your job to *listen.* By doing so, you'll get invaluable information you can use to improve your performance and reputation. If you hear a perception you don't like, don't get defensive: just put together a plan to turn that perception around. In addition to providing great information, these conversations will help you build richer relationships with your colleagues. By reaching out to others for input, you show that you respect them—and people like feeling valued. You also send the message that you are action oriented and interested in growth and development (always a good message to get into the marketplace). And these conversations give you a chance to share with others what you want to do and how you want to be seen, which can shape their perception of you moving forward. Thus, these conversations help you gather information as well as educate others about your goals, and they ultimately enlist support.

These conversations help you gather information as well as educate others about your goals, and they ultimately enlist support.

This really works for George. Lee's perspective was an important motivator. So after doing his own assessment, George reaches out to colleagues for input to help him better articulate the value he adds. In the conversations that follow, he discovers that people value his ability to translate complex numbers into meaningful, easy-to-understand information—information that genuinely helps them make better decisions. He finds that people trust him and also trust that his work will be accurate, thorough, and thoughtful. He learns that while his CPA might be an important credential, it isn't a differentiator—*thousands* of people pass the CPA exams each year. In the end he discovers that what makes him unique is his ability to dig into the numbers and extract the real value; he can translate complex data into understandable and actionable information essential to the leadership team's decisions. And he learns that he's dynamite at leading systems conversion projects. This information helps him uncover ways to position himself more clearly.

Set a Goal

You need some sort of goal, even just a short-term goal, in order to focus your efforts. Different goals require different strategies. For example, if your goal is to move up in your organization, then you need to find a way to make your leadership skills visible to those up the chain. If your goal is not a promotion but rather to just keep your job, keep current in your profession, and get recognized for the value you create, your strategy would focus on making different skills and capabilities visible. In both cases you want the leaders in the organization to know you, but for different reasons. Specific reputations open specific doors. So, what door do you want to open? What is one of your goals? Here are some questions that will help you zero in on a goal.

- Do you want to advance in your current company?
- Would you like to find a new job at a different company?
- Do you want to expand your current responsibilities so you can learn more and become more competent or more marketable, or so you can just enjoy your work more?
- Do you want different assignments so you can explore other career options?
- Do you want to move from an individual contributor role to a supervisory role?
- Do you want to change careers completely or move into a different industry?
- Would you like to get on a corporate or nonprofit board?
- Do you want to move into consulting as a profession?
- Do you want to explore the purchase of a business or franchise?
- Or do you just want to keep your current job as long as you can and keep enjoying it?

Don't worry if you don't have a long-term goal right away. You can make great progress by simply picking a shorter-range goal. This allows you to start taking action right away, today. That lets you get momentum while you figure out additional goals.

Define What You Want to Be Known For

Once you know how you are seen and what your goals are, decide what you want to be known for so you can cultivate a reputation that opens the doors you want opened. As you figure out your own positioning, keep the following recommendations in mind.

- Don't be defined by your current job and company. The most common response to "What do you do?" is a job title and company name: "I'm a business systems analyst at Stasis Enterprises." It isn't wrong to inform people of this, but it doesn't tell people much about what you do or what makes you unique. Don't stop at the title.
- Go beyond, describing your expertise. Focus on the things you're good at—the expertise you offer: "I'm a marketing leader with strengths in understanding customers, crafting key messages, designing advertising and promotion campaigns, leading people, and working with cross-functional teams to implement large-scale change."
- Highlight outcomes and benefits. This is the difference between describing the features of a product and describing the benefits of the product. The features are the things a product does. The benefits are the difference the features make for the user. How does this apply to a person? Let's take George. A feature (an expertise) he might highlight is his ability to simplify processes (an example being a recent project where he reduced a process from ten to four steps). But the benefit (or the outcome) of this feature is that this increased efficiency leads to cost savings (and substantial ones!).

Take a minute and think about what difference you make in your organization. What types of outcomes do you want to stress?

How to Shift What You're Known For

What if your reputation is already very strong, but you don't want to continue doing what you're doing? You need a reputation for other skills. This is fairly common early in a career when an individual contributor wants to move into a supervisory role.

If this is the case for you—for example, if you haven't supervised and you'd like to move into a supervisory role—you need to find opportunities to demonstrate your skills and to educate leadership about what you can really do. Here's a glimpse of the actions you might implement as proof points that help others see you as ready to take on supervision.

- Take a course on supervision, even if it is not sponsored by your company, and share what you're learning.
- Volunteer at a nonprofit in a role where you supervise others; ideally, get feedback so you learn and grow, and get references.
- Research and write an article about how to give feedback (this could be based on taking a class on supervision).
- Write a book review for your company's internal website—and of course, pick a book on some aspect of supervision.
- Talk with your boss or another leader in the company about your interests, and seek their advice.

What actions should Mei take in her situation? Her only work experience has been in service and administrative assistant roles, but she wants to get into human resources. She needs to know what *experiences and skills* are required to be able to do the job. She also needs to think about what *reputation* is important in order to be seen as a human resources professional because that's not the way most people would see her now.

After thinking about it, she realizes that as a waitperson she has demonstrated a lot of customer service skills. She's performed admin work at several organizations, so she knows how organizations work. She's done a lot of research on "best places to work" and how such reputations relate to human resources. She's exploring writing a blog about employee engagement (a strategy you'll learn more about later in this book). And she joins a special interest group focused on best places to work.

If Mei told you about thc work she's doing to educate herself outside her service role, would it change your opinion of how well she would do in a human resources role? We're betting that it would! Throughout this book we will explore many more actions you can take to elevate your visibility around a particular skill or competency. Remember, however, that before you start promoting yourself, you need to know *how* you want to be seen—that is, what you want to be known for.

CRAFT YOUR VALUE PROPOSITION

Now it's time to pull all your thinking and feedback into a statement that articulates your value. Yep, that's why we call it a value proposition; in branding lingo we might call it your brand promise. What can people expect you to deliver? Here's how to turn your thinking and research into a statement you can use to help influence how you are seen and therefore what opportunities come your way.

We won't pretend that defining what you really deliver is easy. It takes time to come up with a great value proposition. First, it requires clarity about what you do and what value you add. Then it demands something that differentiates you from your competitors. You need to sit down and think about this. Consider these questions when crafting your value proposition.

- What value do I add for clients or customers?
- What benefits do my clients/customers/colleagues receive because of what I do?
- What are my unique gifts and talents?
- How have I used them to make a contribution?
- What differentiates me from my peers?

Take some time to explore these questions, and then distill your answers into a short sentence or two. If you can't describe your contributions in a concise and compelling way, how do you expect others to share the word about you? Tactful self-promotion depends on others' being able to share your value proposition.

Focus on Key Outcomes

Start by focusing on the core outcomes you produce—the value you add. It's no mystery what types of outcomes companies care about:

- **Increases or improvement in**: revenue, profit, market share, share of wallet, brand recognition, customer experience, customer satisfaction, bottom line, morale, engagement, efficiency, productivity, customer retention, employee retention, quality of decision making, speed to market, etc.
- **Reduction in**: cost, turnover, rework, safety violations, accidents, etc.
- **Avoidance of**: risk, penalties and fines, legal actions against the company, etc.

Jot down some ideas of what your work might look like when described in the above terms. The language may feel stiff, but they will help you see yourself from the company's point of view. What makes you an asset or resource? That's part of your value. Once you know what the company is getting out of the deal, rephrase it to match your own personality and style.

Here are a few examples to prime the pump and get you thinking about your own value proposition:

- "My goal is to work as a sound engineer. For the last eight years, I've been playing keyboard in a band. I'm the guy who sets up the equipment, and if something goes wrong, I tinker with it and get it fixed. My degree in physics comes in handy here. I work in engineering to make money, but I love music, and I love making it sound great."
- "I'm a receptionist who makes sure that every customer, employee, or vendor who calls or comes through the door has a positive first impression of our company. You might call me the 'director of first impressions.'"

- "I'm an operations leader with a history of building new infrastructures and tweaking old ones to increase efficiency, improve employee engagement, and enhance the customer experience."
- "I'm a senior executive who builds technology businesses that stand the test of time."
- "My specialty as an OD consultant is creating high-engagement cultures—basically, creating an environment that employees can't wait to get to in the morning and don't want to leave at night."
- "I'm a sales leader with a history of inspiring teams to top performance. The outcome? Growing market share and profitability, even in the toughest markets."

You can see how each examples stresses not a skill set, but an outcome: the results that the person delivers for the organization. Granted, they may not be all that exciting, but the first step is simply being clear about the value you deliver to an organization. We'll figure out how to make it more intriguing later.

If you're still feeling stuck, here's an alternative approach to describing your outcomes. You can follow a simple template to create a more conversational version. Once you know this format, you can improvise on it as you find yourself talking with different people. The key is to think a little in advance so you are not caught off guard when asked that inevitable question: "What do you do?" Here is the template:

- "You know we've had this [*describe problem, challenge, opportunity, or goal*].
- My role is to [*solve that problem, capitalize on that opportunity, etc.*]
- by [*describe actions*], so that [*describe outcome*]."

The following samples build on the template and place the outcomes into more context.

- "You know how you get really irritated when your e-mail goes down or you can't print a document? When that happens to one person, it's a pain. When it happens to a hundred people, it's costly—it takes a toll on productivity and morale. I run the department that makes sure your technology is always working for you—to save you the headache and save the company a bundle."

- "I'm sure you're aware of how social media is changing the way people buy stuff—how they research and choose products, where they shop, and how they make purchasing decisions. I'm in marketing, and marketing as a discipline is trying to figure out how to respond to this trend. Companies that figure it out will reap great rewards; those that don't will fall behind. I'm an executive who retools marketing departments to keep companies current and ensure that they take advantage of this huge opportunity."

Add Proof to Your Value Proposition

One way to increase the impact of your statement is to be ready with proof, especially examples of accomplishments that back up your claim. Here is an example of a statement that includes some proof.

> "I'm a marketing consultant who helps organizations take advantage of social media. Most companies are losing a ton of money by experimenting without really knowing what they are doing. I provide clarity, focus, and direction to their efforts—and I typically get a twenty-five percent return on investment within the first three months of an engagement."
>
> Providing a specific example of an outcome when stating your value proposition isn't always possible or necessary, but it can be very powerful.

Make Your Value Proposition Conversational

Knowing your value proposition is important. It is part of what you want to be known for—being the one who solves the toughest technical challenges, or who knows how to squeeze the most profit out of a value chain, or who organizes information to make life better for everyone else. But how do you share this information with others? There are many ways, but we want you to be tactful about it. There is no need to force your statement on others. Just have it ready when opportunities present themselves. When someone asks what you do or what your job is, that's when you can pull out your value proposition.

You'll want a very short, catchy version for when you're at a party or a bar or when you run into someone on the street. It aims to encourage people to ask questions if they're interested. For example, a few of the value propositions mentioned above might be shortened to:

- "I make music sound better."
- "I tame the Internet to make more sales."
- "I'm the director of first impressions."
- "I help companies be better places to work."

Here are some guidelines to consider when you start putting your proposition together.

- **Does it resonate with your target audience?** You need to know your target audience—for example, entrepreneurs, CFOs, marketing professionals, IT geeks—and what they care about. While your message should be broad enough that most people can understand what you do, it needs to be focused on things of critical interest to your audience.
- **Is it authentic?** While you want your statement to focus on others' interests, it also needs to tap into your genuine passions and excitement about what you do. You want to talk about things you love. Only by tapping into this will you be able to deliver your message with enthusiasm.
- **Is it clear?** The rule of thumb is not to use language past an eighth-grade level; some say a fifth-grade level. This just means to keep it simple. No need to use big words when smaller ones will do. You're not trying to impress with jargon or sophisticated vocabulary. You're just trying to be clear.

- **Is it compelling?** This means picking words that tell a story or paint a picture. For example, this statement is pretty dull: "I work well with people at all levels of an organization." By adding, "from the shop floor to the executive suite," you create a picture in the listener's mind and bring a dull statement to life. Another example is from an executive we worked with who prided himself on his candor. When we asked him what made him a great CEO, he claimed it was his ability to "cut through the bull and address the core issues." Actually, he used even more vivid language than this, and we never forgot it!
- **Is it easy to share with others?** You want to be known for something, and the way that reputation spreads is through others. You can have some influence on what is said about you if you can supply a repeatable idea. Don't get too complex or clever. The primary purpose of your statement is to communicate to others what value you offer in a way that they remember and can repeat to others. That's the best test of a good statement. Try yours out on friends and family until you get it right.

Creating this type of statement takes work and often some brainstorming with friends or colleagues. This is what Natasha does. At lunch with a couple of trusted colleagues, she asks for help. One idea builds on another, and she ends up with some great phrases.

Natasha knows that she wants to reference both new and old products, so she starts by expanding on this idea: "Not only do I come up with new product ideas, but I'm particularly good at polishing old products and creating profitable line extensions." This is true but not too compelling. One colleague, Joshua, chimes in, "You build teams that polish old products and add profitability to the brand." Well, that has more of a leadership feel to it. After still more noodling, Natasha comes up with something she really likes that gets her colleagues nodding in agreement: "I lead teams that launch game-changing products and breathe new life into legacy product lines." She feels she's getting close to something she can confidently share with others.

Henry is also making progress. He wrote down phrases from his performance appraisals and from friends' comments. He highlighted key phrases, and ideas started to emerge. He came up with: "I'm a software developer known for spotting problems early in the development cycle, which means they get fixed before they get out of control. This helps my team consistently release software on schedule with rarely a single glitch." Henry is starting to feel better about his prospects.

George, the finance consultant, has always received praise from his internal customers about being a good listener who builds great relationships and seems to understand the issues of various stakeholders, which is especially helpful when implementing big changes, such as shifting to new systems. He's found that the obstacles to a successful transition are more about people's resistance than technical issues. So he uses his people skills to help ensure these transitions are smooth and that the people affected by the changes are well informed and involved throughout the process. But when he describes this to people, they don't seem to get how important it is.

What's the outcome of George's people skills? As he thinks on this question, he realizes that his good people skills help him implement changes smoothly. He thinks he's on to something, but he's not sure it's very powerful. He goes back to the core questions of who his clients will be and what they want from a finance consultant. His primary audience is not the managers who have to implement the system, but rather the leaders who want the new system to work, for people to use it, and for it to deliver the value it promises. His client is really the whole finance department and its leader. He realizes that the finance leader wants a lot more than a consultant who merely gets along with people.

George realizes he's been thinking about *how* he does his job, not the outcomes of his work. So when he asked the right question, he got a different answer: What do leaders really want? They want the system to work, and they don't want to hear a lot of complaints about it. George thinks he's got it. He quickly jots down, "I work with finance departments that want a flawless transition from their legacy finance system to a new system, so they get the bottom-line results they are planning for, and not a lot of noise about it." He thinks the leaders will respond to this. Next, when he's asked how he accomplishes flawless transitions, he explains how his people skills and collaborative approach with stakeholders lead to a smooth process. He believes that now he has a much stronger way to position himself in the market.

Mei has also been working on her value proposition. She realizes she has a history of helping make her work area more fun and more efficient, a place where people want to be. The paper she was proudest of in school was about HR strategies proven effective at creating cultures that helped organizations get on the "best places to work" list. She identified three core practices that were consistent among 80 percent of the companies on the list, so she could talk with some confidence about this aspect of HR strategy. Her friends work for companies that talk a lot about becoming places that attract and retain top talent, yet it always surprises Mei to hear that those companies rarely align with these best practices. She thinks she might have a hook here. Her draft statement reads, "Companies talk a lot about becoming the 'best place to work.' I'm excited about combining my years of study of HR best practices with my on-the-ground customer service experience to make this ideal not just a promise but a reality." When she feels bold, perhaps she'll say, "You might say I put the *human* in human resources" (tongue in cheek, of course). She plans to keep working on it, but she feels she can start testing it out to see if it resonates with her target audience.

Write Your Own Value Proposition

Now it's your turn. Take a stab at crafting your own statement. Before moving on to the next chapter, take a few minutes to capture your thinking about your own value proposition. Don't worry at this point about making it perfect; just strive for something you can try out on trusted colleagues and friends. You can tweak it later, based on people's reactions.

Ultimately, whatever you come up with needs to sound natural, not scripted. When asked what you do, part of your brand is conveyed not in *what* you say but in *how* you say it. Let people see your enthusiasm. It's intoxicating, and it motivates others to both remember what you say and pass it on to others. We suggest you write out your statement, at least in bullet points, and then practice it until it feels comfortable. The more you say it out loud, the more comfortable you'll be when an opportunity to share it arises.

When asked what you do, part of your brand is conveyed not in ***what*** *you say but in* ***how*** *you say it.*

So, now you should know the core value you are promoting. You aren't promoting yourself, per se; you are promoting the *value* you deliver. It's important to take the time to articulate your value now, because your value proposition is a vital foundation for the rest of our strategies.

TAKE ACTION TO POWER YOUR CAREER

Most people need work on their brand and value proposition, and most find it challenging. But the effort will pay off!

- Do some self-reflection about your brand and your goals. Consider talking with your colleagues about your brand: What are your strengths? What makes you unique?

- Identify the types of outcomes you deliver or the differences you make, and craft a statement to describe this brand promise. Revise it. Refine it. Revise it. Refine it.
- Practice this statement out loud, often, and get comfortable describing your value in a consistent way.

CHAPTER 3

SHARE ACCOMPLISHMENTS AND LEARNINGS

If you done it, it ain't braggin.

–Will Rogers

By this point, our four friends are feeling better—they have begun to identify their value and have crafted value propositions that are taking shape, even if they are not final. But they haven't yet found the right moments to share these statements in daily conversation. When Natasha chats with a VP who asks how things are going, she doesn't see a way to easily launch into her value proposition—and that's normal, because these statements don't usually work inside your own organization. When Henry runs into a friend at a party, he isn't comfortable spouting his either. Clearly there is a time and a place for the formal value statements, but our four friends need something else to say in more casual conversations. They needed more tools in their toolkits.

To get known in your own organization, you need to talk about something you've accomplished, something you've learned, or something you're working on that is relevant to your business and goals.

Your value proposition makes a promise, but you need to reinforce that promise on a regular basis. The answer is to make sure you are consistently doing things that demonstrate your value, proving that you actually deliver results. We call these accomplishments.

Make sure you are consistently doing things that demonstrate your value, proving that you actually deliver results.

There are two important ideas here. First, you have to get into the habit of thinking about what you do to add value to your organization or profession. Each day, each week, each month, can you answer the question of what you do to add value to or further the goals of your organization? If you answer yes, then the hard work is done. Second, you need to get those accomplishments noticed by others. And we've got several ideas for how to do this.

TELL PEOPLE WHAT YOU'RE WORKING ON (OR WHAT YOU'RE LEARNING)

We know this sounds really simple. And you know why? Because it *is* really simple. And it may be the most important suggestion we make in this entire book. This habit alone, consistently executed over time, can transform how others see you.

Take advantage of this most missed opportunity. How many times a day do you get asked, "How's it going?" or "What's going on?" or something along those lines? And how do you respond? Do you use this moment as an opportunity to educate and inform, or to complain? Questions like that are often examples of what's called "socially reflexive language"—just something to say—and you need to be aware of that context. If someone asks you "How's it going?" by way of greeting rather than interest, don't burden that person with all your woes—no matter how many hours you worked over the weekend.

Sometimes, however, "How's it going?" reflects a genuine interest in what is happening. The very first story shared in this book explains Richard's real-world experience when his colleague Laura shared an accomplishment with their boss and Richard shared only that he was doing fine. As Richard tells this story, Laura later challenged him, "What are you thinking? You're doing all this great work—how do you expect him to know it if you don't tell him?" Sure enough: when their boss continued down the hall, he knew the value Laura was contributing but not what Richard was doing.

Think about the value you're adding or what you're working on. To do this well, you need to be adding value and you need to know what story you want to communicate about that value. Then you need to tell that story when the opportunity comes up. Now, you don't have to respond with an accomplishment statement every time someone asks you how you're doing. That would get old fast. But when you interact with people who matter, we suspect you could share more about what you do. So, when someone asks, "How are you doing?" don't respond with "Oh, fine" or worse, a complaint about being overworked. Instead, share an accomplishment: "I'm great—I just resolved a bug in the system that should save everyone a lot of headaches." No exaggeration is necessary—simply tell people what you have achieved.

No exaggeration is necessary—simply tell people what you have achieved.

If talking about this type of accomplishment feels too pretentious for you, talk about what you're doing—it may not be as impressive as an accomplishment, but it still promotes you and lets people know more about you. For example, you could say, "I'm working on the Neptune project, and right now we're trying to work through the problem of getting two systems to talk with each other." Or, "I was just asked to join a task force working on customer relationship management. We're still in the early stages, but it's fascinating, and it's broadening my horizon." Or if you're in the job hunt, say, "I just finished my value proposition, and now I'm beginning to make contact with a lot of former coworkers."

Consider what you're learning. In addition to sharing accomplishments, talking about what you're learning is very appealing to a listener. You can express enthusiasm, and it may inspire others to think a bit as well, which is energizing for them. If someone asks you about a day of training or a conference you recently attended, don't just comment on the food or the location. Mention something specific you learned and are applying at work. For example, you could respond, "I just got back from a conference where I learned some ways to help us be more efficient—it was terrific!" People will start to see you as a learner who strives to improve things, and they will begin to associate you with the skills you talk about. Adapt this idea to a tone, style, and language comfortable for you and suited for your listener.

Let your (good) attitude show. Showing energy and enthusiasm in your response is important. This is a great opportunity to demonstrate your passion for your work and model the kind of behavior that leads to a great reputation. You get to choose the topic, so pick something you are genuinely excited about. And let your positive attitude show! We'll have more to say about presence in the next chapter, but it's important to mention here that your reputation is based not only on the content of your response but also on how you say it. If you blather on in a monotone about the success of a project, you won't make a positive impression. Be brief, be energized, and then ask how the other person is doing.

Help others see the skills you want them to see. What if you are trying to become known for something other than the skills required for your core job? In this case, don't talk about the mundane tasks you focus on all day. Instead, mention something you're doing on a volunteer basis, or talk about something you've learned that's relevant to how you want to be seen. For example, if you are interested in being seen as supervisory material, but no one knows your skills in this area, you might let them know about the training you've taken or a book or TED talk on leadership you recently encountered that got you excited.

Natasha started using this strategy after she attended a Global Business conference. It took place in Buenos Aires, and after the conference she visited a customer in the region to learn more about their operation. She was excited to talk about what she learned, and there was a lot she could talk about. But her goal was to be seen more as a global leader, so she talked about the experience in ways that not only excited her but also helped establish the reputation she needed.

Entrepreneurs and freelancers can use this technique as well. If you're a solo practitioner, you'll field a lot of questions about how your business is going, and you'll need to respond with energy. If things are going well, offer an example of a project you find exciting, ideally one with a great result. If things aren't going quite as well as you'd hoped, consider using one of Nancy's standbys: "In fact, I'm right where I planned to be." She might have revised her business plan that morning, but as of this moment, she's on plan. Say it as she does, with verve.

George doesn't have any business yet, so he has felt uncomfortable when others have asked how things are going. But after shifting his focus, he now comes up with this: "Things are going well. I've been talking with a lot of people, and they seem excited about my approach to system conversions. I've got proposals out, meetings on the calendar—I'm feeling good. And how are things going with you?"

You get the idea. This isn't a complicated strategy. It's a habit, and as such it gets easier the more you do it. Think regularly about what you're doing to add value and what you're learning. Then put that knowledge into language and share it now and again. Give this a try today and see the difference it can make.

If you're conducting a job search, you definitely need to be ready. When you're on the job hunt, the question is ubiquitous: "How is your job search going?" And job seekers often share more than they should. Be strategic and respond with the most positive statement you can while still telling the truth. It's easy to complain because the search is hard—"Well, it's a marathon, and I can't wait until it's over." But will the listener want to keep talking to this person?

Henry comes up with two responses, depending on the situation. The first is for general situations: "The job search is going well. I'm meeting a lot of very interesting people and learning a lot about the local market. The right opportunity hasn't materialized yet, but I'm optimistic about my prospects." This is a person people will want to talk with. They may follow up with questions about what the "right opportunity" would be, or they may ask what he's learning about the local market. You can use such responses to your advantage in a conversation. His other response is most appropriate for fellow IT professionals: "Things are great—I've been using some of my time to step back and look at what skills I really want to use. And I've been learning a whole lot about Cloud technology and the Internet of Things. It's really interesting, and I'm hoping to find work that allows me to continue to explore these interests."

Henry had a breakthrough when he was asked whether he was looking for permanent or temporary work. He had practiced using positive phrases as responses to questions, so he was prepared to say, "I don't care about the title—it's all about the kind of work that I can do. I want to work on cutting-edge technology and things that interest me." He realized this was true. In his previous role, he didn't have the chance to use cutting-edge technology, so he didn't want to get stuck in that situation again. He'd initially been thinking about looking for permanent work, but he realized that contract gigs might offer him the chance to do more interesting, forward-looking work.

The key here, as in other scenarios, is to take a couple of minutes to think about what you will say before you walk into a situation where you're likely to be asked about your job search.

Accomplishment Stories for Interviewing

Job interviews are perfect times to share your accomplishments. Interviews give you an opportunity to share them in more detail, but you don't want to ramble on either. It helps to have stories prepared. Henry learned this the hard way. He was asked in an interview about a time when he went "above and beyond." He had to think about it. After a little bit of fumbling, he said he was always willing to work overtime. On the drive home from the interview, he thought perhaps he hadn't prepared as well as he should have. He talked with friends who had recently gone through job searches, and they shared how they had answered interview questions with stories about their accomplishments.

The pattern they described was pretty simple: explain the *situation*, share what *actions* you took, and then reveal the *results* you achieved. We call this the S-A-R story structure. Having a structure helps Henry create several stories he can share with confidence in interviews. He starts by revisiting the accomplishments he had identified when reviewing his performance appraisals, and then he chooses a few that best support his value proposition.

THE S-A-R STORY STRUCTURE

Situation—Describe the situation you were in. What problem were you solving? What was the purpose of the project or assignment? What was at risk if it didn't go well? What challenges did you face?

Action—Describe what you did. What specific actions did you take to move the project or initiative forward?

Result—Describe the outcome of the project. What difference did it make to the organization (revenue, savings, customer satisfaction, employee engagement, etc.)?

Here is Henry's story about a time he went above and beyond what was expected. He feels it is a much stronger answer.

> "Our company had a chance to bid on a large project, but the bid had to be in on Monday. People were pretty disappointed because we didn't seem to have the time to create the technical documents needed for the proposal. So I volunteered to work through the weekend if necessary to help out. They took me up on it, and it turned out to be even more work than we thought. But I partnered with the sales person and created everything we needed. We got the proposal in on time and were asked to present. The head of sales invited me to the meeting as a technical resource. We won the business. They turned into a pretty big client for us over the last two years."

When creating and using your own S-A-R stories, keep these tips in mind:

- Make bullets for each S-A-R story. Don't write a script; you just need the key ideas fleshed out. Every time you tell a story, it will come out differently, and it should. But think through the organization and key ideas in advance.

- Keep the stories focused and relatively short (under one minute). If you have a story that takes too long to tell, it's likely because there are a lot of stories packed in there. So create a high-level overview story: sketch the big picture and then craft sub-stories about different aspects of the project.

- If you're preparing for an interview, take a look at the job description and the competencies required. Make sure you have stories to show how you've used those competencies in the past to make a difference.

- Practice your stories out loud. Really. We mean it. You can *think* about these stories all you want, but they never come out of your mouth exactly as you thought they would. So say them aloud several times. The more you practice the stories, the more comfortable you'll be telling them in an interview.

COMMUNICATE WITH YOUR BOSS

It's important to take advantage of impromptu moments when your boss asks how you're doing, but you can't rely entirely on informal methods of self-promotion with a relationship this important. You need to be deliberate about ensuring that your boss notices your accomplishments. Here are some actions you can take.

Schedule Periodic One-on-Ones

Even if it isn't standard operating procedure, set up regular meetings with your boss. For many this is a weekly meeting. For others it makes more sense to meet every other week or even once a month. The general purpose of these meetings is to make sure you are aligned with your boss's goals and that you are getting the help you need to exceed expectations. But it is your job to use this time to update your boss about your accomplishments or progress on your goals. Of course, you can also discuss what you're learning and how this knowledge or skill is helping you produce results. Many of us let the boss drive the conversation in these one-on-ones, but this is a time for you to speak up and educate your boss. Take some time to plan before the meeting, so you're ready to shine.

Provide Periodic Written Updates

Even if you don't meet with your boss on a regular basis, you can provide regular progress updates in writing. This way, your boss always knows what's going on and is never surprised by a stalled project or slipped deadline (thanks to being constantly in the loop about challenges). Even if your boss doesn't ask for it, providing a regular update (weekly, monthly, or quarterly) will ensure that your boss knows the value you're adding.

The nice thing about this strategy is that *you* shape the story and can clarify the results or benefits of the work you are doing. And you can stress your accomplishments and learning, which are true benefits to the company as well as means to shape the reputation you want to cultivate. For instance, if you want to be seen as a potential supervisor, make sure you have a section in your update about a book you've read, a course you've taken, or a skill you've been practicing that supports this goal.

Actively Shape Your Performance Review

Performance reviews are a standard part of the yearly evaluation and planning process. Most of us approach them with little enthusiasm. But they are an opportunity to highlight your accomplishments and learning. If you take the advice offered above, then your review will be a slam dunk. Your boss will receive periodic written updates, which you will discuss in regularly scheduled meetings. In this ideal scenario, your boss can then pack your review with concrete information about the differences you made to your company. In fact, it's a good idea to write up your own summary of your accomplishments for the year, with tangible measures for results if possible, and submit this summary in advance. This makes your boss's job easier. No one likes to write performance reviews, which means much of what you write may end up in your file. You have a lot more control over your review than you might imagine. It just takes some planning and consistent execution, and it's a lot more effective if you make sharing accomplishments a habit throughout the year.

Although freelancers and people in temporary jobs don't usually have performance reviews, it is worth keeping a record of what you've accomplished. Mei was in this situation for a few years while she did temp administrative and service jobs. When she got a note from a customer on her good service or an e-mail that said something nice about her work, she filed it away. It gave her a record of the many good things she had done, which helped her immensely when she was writing her résumé and trying to determine her brand and value proposition. Every worker—temporary or "permanent"—

should be in the habit of doing this for performance reviews and other career needs.

In a later chapter, we'll discuss other ideas for getting your boss on your side, making your leader look good, and cultivating advocates among your higher-ups. For now, we are just trying to make sure that your boss knows what you are up to and the value you are adding. This means you're scheduling periodic one-on-ones, providing updates, and taking responsibility for the content in your performance review. These three strategies can make a big difference.

ELEVATE COMPLIMENTS

Another strategy for making sure your accomplishments are noticed is to make it easy for others to pass on the good news about the difference you're making. Just as in the first strategy—telling people what you're doing when they ask, "What's up?"—this strategy is about taking advantage of opportunities as they arise.

Leverage Compliments from Customers or Colleagues

If you're doing good work for a customer, they may well tell you so. You know when a customer (internal or external) is happy with what you've delivered. Sometimes they say it out loud: "Julie, thanks so much. You've really gone the extra mile, and we really appreciate it. Is there anything I can do for you?" And you know what we want you to say to that! "As a matter of fact, yes! It would be great if you'd send a note to my boss to let her know you were satisfied with my work. Would you be willing to do that?" It isn't so hard. And your customers will be happy to do it—it will take them three minutes to send the e-mail, and they'll feel good about it. And your boss will know that you're delivering!

Forward Complimentary E-mails to Your Boss

What do you do if you get an e-mail of thanks from a customer or colleague? Again, you know where we're headed. Simply forward it on to your boss (and perhaps another key stakeholder or two) with a note to give it context. Something like, "Just wanted to let you know we're in good shape with the Juniper project—I just got this note from Lee." Or, "I thought you'd be happy to learn that Kelley feels good about the service their department is getting. After all the work our team has done to deliver on this account, it feels really good to get this acknowledgment." Or something as simple as, "FYI—another happy customer!" You don't need to position or comment. Even just "FYI" by itself will do. The key is to make sure a positive note gets into the right hands.

Natasha decided to get into this habit, and not just on things she did herself. She began to forward e-mails she received complimenting her team members as well, thereby elevating both herself and her team. In addition, she reached out to her boss's peers. When one of her staff got a positive e-mail from the sales group, she e-mailed the VP of sales and added a cover note: "I really appreciate this note from one of your team members—they are great at collaborating with us."

Of course, to be tactful, you need to be selective. You probably don't need to send your boss notes every day. But the really big ones, the ones from important clients or key stakeholders, should not be your secret affirmations—they should see the light of day, and only you can make that happen by hitting forward. And don't forget to save the note in an e-mail folder, or even print it and place it in a paper folder, ready for use when preparing for your performance review.

Ask for Recommendations

To make an accomplishment even more visible and to gain exposure with a larger audience, consider asking for a recommendation on LinkedIn. Again, this is something you would request after you have built a relationship and a track record of consistently delivering results. But too often we pass on opportunities to make this request. Even if you feel you've missed a perfect opportunity in a conversation, it's never too late. Send an e-mail. For instance, Mei wrote,

> *"Hi Aisha. I was just thinking about the positive remarks you made about my work today, and it got me thinking. I've been trying to build my reputation online, and I wondered if you'd feel comfortable writing a brief testimonial about your experience working with me—nothing long, just a sentence or two. Is this something you might consider? If it would help you, I'll draft something that you can revise. Thanks in advance."*

Of course there are many ways to ask that will work well. The point is to *ask*.

We bet there are a dozen people you could ask for a testimonial right now. Pick just one and try it out. It will work! We'll provide more tips for securing and leveraging testimonials in the later chapter on LinkedIn. For now, we wanted to mention it as a tactic for elevating accomplishments.

TAKE ACTION TO POWER YOUR CAREER

Building a track record of success is important, but so is sharing what you've accomplished or what you're learning. Key ideas include:

- Make a habit of thinking about what you're working on, what differences you're making, and what message you want to send to others. Be ready with a recent example to share. Jot down two things you would say if you were asked today.
- Find ways to make sure your boss knows what you're contributing. Make a plan.
- Start a performance file in which to save everything you want to remember about your performance and contributions.
- Be deliberate about making sure the good work you're doing gets documented and shared by simply asking others to speak up.

CHAPTER 4

PROJECT A POWERFUL PRESENCE

Clothes and manners do not make the man;
but when he is made, they greatly improve his appearance.
—Arthur Ashe

Developing your brand, your value proposition, and your accomplishment stories is strategic and critical. However, a big part of your brand is the impression you make on others through your presence and image. People can't read inside you: they can only assume your brand by what they see and hear on the outside. What's on the outside needs to reflect what's inside the package.

Energy. Enthusiasm. Confidence. Charisma. Professionalism. These words are often used to describe presence and image, but they are difficult concepts to measure and act on. How do you project confidence? How do you look professional? How do you get noticed in your work setting yet still be yourself? When it comes to presence, it seems the only thing people say is, "I know it when I see it." True, perhaps, but not helpful.

Think about a time when someone walked into a gathering and everyone immediately took notice of that person. What did that person do, or how did he or she appear that gave off that power? People like this are often not the most attractive in the room, but they clearly stand out . . . Why?

In this chapter we will cover some of the basics of presence and appearance so you can use them to support the work you have done with your brand and value proposition.

Polishing your positioning statement—so that you are aware of your strengths and value and what you are promoting—should give you good reason to walk into a room with confidence. There are also many small things you can do that have a big impact.

PRESENCE

We'll start with presence, the more strategic of the two concepts. It has to do with projecting confidence, power (in a good way), and approachability.

In her book *The Charisma Myth*, Olivia Fox Cabane defines presence in a way that many of us don't think about: being totally present to others, keeping your attention and complete focus on them. She also talks about power (whether a person has the ability to help us) and warmth (whether that person wants to use that power to help us). Cabane believes that, contrary to popular belief, charisma isn't something "you have or you don't have." She breaks charisma down into a series of behaviors that anyone can develop. Similarly, Jeffrey Pfeffer, in his book *Power: Why Some People Have It—and Others Don't*, outlines personal qualities that lead to power and presence. Along with ambition, focus, and confidence, he includes qualities such as empathy—not always what we think of when we think of power, but very important when it comes to connecting with and influencing others. Even if you've never felt particularly charismatic, we argue that presence isn't just something you're born with, but something you can cultivate. Here are some ways to get started.

Know Yourself!

Be comfortable with who you are, but also be aware of how you come across to others. Do an honest self-assessment. The first step to making a positive impression is to know yourself and to ensure that your external appearance and conduct put your best (but still honest) self forward. You aren't trying to cover up who you are. You want to be yourself! But to be authentically yourself, you must know yourself.

The first step to making a positive impression is to know yourself and to ensure that your external appearance and conduct put your best (but still honest) self forward.

Authenticity cannot be a costume—if you try to "put on" authenticity, it won't work. Look around at those who have the type of presence you wish to convey. How do they do it? How can you be authentic and also build warm relationships? And how does this align with self-promotion? For example, if you're shy and introverted, you can't become the boisterous life of the party—that ain't you! Rather than trying to be someone you're not, you need to find approaches that enable you to more comfortably interact with other people. This may include using conversation starters, open-ended questions, sincere compliments, a positioning statement that is "you," and other approaches suggested throughout this book.

Posture

Use body language to show confidence, authority, presence, and warmth. In addition to projecting confidence and power, you want to appear approachable. Body posture determines how you feel and act, not just how you are perceived. If you are slumped physically, you are likely to be slumped mentally. Muscles, in particular, and the body, in general, are associated with very specific feelings. Your body can drive your emotions as much as your emotions can drive your body.

Amy Cuddy, in her powerful 2012 TED talk, "Your Body Language Shapes Who You Are," illustrates how different stances not only project more personal power but also change how powerful we feel inside. A social psychologist, she says it's not "fake it 'til you make it," it's "fake it 'til you become it!" She's not suggesting that you be inauthentic. But changing a few habits can help you *be* more powerful in a way that works for you. Authentically.

POWER POSTURE EXERCISE

Try this exercise as a first step: stand erect, arms out, and project energy! You don't have to be a professional model to adopt excellent posture: put your head up and your shoulders back, and increase your share of space in the room. Keep your arms unfolded; open arms make it easier for others to approach you.

Smile!

What's your natural expression? Do you naturally smile and appear welcoming and approachable, or is your natural look aloof, grumpy, or unsure? Get feedback from others.

A smile has to be genuine. Ultimately, people will know if you're faking it. If smiling doesn't feel natural for you, think about what does make you smile. Your sense of enjoyment shows when you're engaged in something. You can help yourself by doing some positive self-talk. Think about this when you're heading into an important meeting or interview with a new contact. If you just paste on a smile you don't feel, it will seem phony to you and to those you're meeting. However, if you engage in some positive self-talk, you can find a more genuine smile (and a better mood in general). Instead of focusing on how much you hate to interview or how important this is, tell yourself, "I will enjoy meeting this new person and learning more about her." Practicing this positive self-talk will help you project a sincere smile as your new contact introduces herself.

Smiling not only creates the right impression in others; it also creates the right emotion in you. In one psychology experiment, college students were asked to rate the humor of Gary Larson's *The Far Side* cartoons. One group of subjects was asked to do this with a pencil held horizontally between their teeth. Another group was asked to do this while holding the pencil in their lips. If you try this, you will realize that in the first case you are smiling and in the second case you are frowning. In this experiment, the "smilers" had much more positive ratings of Larson's cartoons than the "frowners," even though these gestures were forced by the pencils in their mouths. Smiling helps you feel this right emotion, which in turn will help you to be genuine in your smile.

Henry, a serious person and an introvert, got feedback in the course of his networking that he had a great sense of humor, but people didn't see it very often. Henry became conscious of smiling as he approached people most of the time, and he let people see the (appropriately) humorous side of him. He found that this gave him more confidence, and he even began to enjoy interacting with other people more.

Eye Contact

Do you look people in the eye and make appropriate eye contact? Good eye contact indicates that you're listening attentively, staying present to the other person. Holding eye contact for too long—staring—can be intimidating and uncomfortable for the other person. Shy people may have more difficulty with this, and other people may have cultural barriers against making eye contact. Get feedback from others, and practice making good eye contact until you feel more comfortable with it.

Nancy remembers a time in her career when the CEO of her company was practicing "managing by walking around"—a management technique recommended by Thomas Peters's popular 1982 book *In Search of Excellence.* Unfortunately, this introverted CEO walked briskly and made no eye contact except with other executives. He didn't get it. While it was nice to see him leave his office more frequently, a few little pauses with eye contact (and perhaps a smile now and then) would have made a big difference in engaging employees. People judge a lot by eye contact. Is yours warm and caring? Anxious? Intimidating?

Handshake

Let's talk about the handshake: it's important for both men and women, and some people don't do it well. It needs to be a firm grasp that projects confidence. Avoid the extremes, whether limp rag or hand-crusher. Some people (mostly men) will grab a woman's fingers rather than grasping the full hand—a real blunder!

Here again, practice is worthwhile. Facing a partner, extend your right hand out in front of you, arm and fingers horizontal, with your fingers together and your thumb upright. Move your hand into your partner's hand, sliding all the way in, until the notch between your thumb and forefinger touches the notch between your partner's thumb and forefinger. Only then do you grasp. Be firm, not crushing. Get feedback from the other person—was it limp-spaghetti-like or painful? Was it the right firmness? Practice this until it comes naturally.

APPEARANCE

A number of years ago, our office had an open position we were trying to fill—in fact, that we were desperate to fill. We received a résumé from someone with a background very close to what we needed. John had the right training, experience, and technical skills. He was available immediately. We couldn't wait to meet him because we thought he was tailor-made for our organization. However, when he arrived for the interview, it didn't take long to see that he was not the kind of person we needed. His clothes were out of date, rumpled, and didn't fit right (though they were probably appropriate twenty-five pounds ago). His shoes were unpolished and scuffed. He needed a haircut. He slouched in his chair. We could see that he had good knowledge, but he didn't project the image we needed to project to customers. We didn't offer him the position, even though we were desperate.

We have also interviewed people who came in barefoot (yes, it's true!) and women with low-cut, revealing tops—all of whom left us wondering, "What were they thinking?!" And it's not just us. A 2013 survey published by OfficeTeam shows that 80 percent of executives said clothing choices affect an employee's chances of earning a promotion. While this figure is down from 93 percent in 2007, it's still something to consider if you're aiming up the ladder!

Whether we like it, image is important in most situations—some more than others. Image is made up of a number of small and big elements, and little things can mean a lot. Look in the mirror. Ask a mentor or friend who will give you honest, helpful feedback. If you're early in your career, feedback is especially helpful. If you're later in your career—let's say, "chronologically gifted"—you may face some special challenges, but it's not too late to seek help on making changes.

We've included a few of the common elements that go into creating your image. Truthfully, whole books have been written about each one of these. We're just bringing them up as reminders. If you feel you need to work on them, seek out additional feedback and other resources on the topics important to you.

Dress and Accessories

How you dress shows respect—or not—for other people as well as for the culture of an organization. In the course of starting his business, George read about an experiment in which a man invested in a range of wardrobe options, from expensive to cheap, and found that the more expensive his clothes were, the more effective he was in making sales. (This is mostly attributable to how much more confident the man felt in the better clothes.) Although George knew he couldn't afford top-of-the-line clothes, he decided to invest in a few really good outfits from someone who was honest about which styles and colors would look best on him. George can't prove that the clothes will result in increased sales, but he feels much more confident walking into meetings, and we can't help but believe this will help him increase his business!

Overdressing can be intimidating and off-putting to others. Underdressing can appear disrespectful and isn't helpful to your career progression, no matter how good your work may be. Look at the people one or two levels up the corporate ladder from you. How do they dress? Consider moving your style of dress in their direction. We have met with many, many people doing some serious networking, and we are frequently shocked to see them coming from an important networking meeting in a sweatshirt!

- When in doubt, overdress. If you're attending a professional meeting, dress a little better than you think you might need to.
- Choose up-to-date clothes that fit your style. Make sure clothes are clean and pressed—even permanent press fabrics often need a touch-up with an iron. (And Millennials—yes, you should own an iron!)
- Wear the right size for your current weight.
- Keep shoes polished and repaired.
- Get a personal shopper to help you select and fit new clothes. It usually doesn't cost extra, and even many thrift shops have people who specialize in helping you pick clothing that looks best on you. Or bring a friend who will give you honest feedback.

Don't forget accessories. They are as important as dress. People will notice and form an opinion about you based on these choices. A few key accessories to pay attention to include:

- Eyeglasses—an accessory you wear out front every day—should be contemporary and clean.
- Jewelry should be appropriate to the occasion and generally understated.
- Scents should be used cautiously, partly because many workplaces have policies against wearing them, and also because there are people who are very sensitive to these chemicals.
- Carry a briefcase or portfolio to convey a businesslike image, rather than grabbing scraps of paper for taking notes. We once watched a woman who appeared to be in a serious networking meeting in a coffee shop. She was wearing a smart white blouse, navy suit, and heels. She was listening intently to her partner—but taking notes on folded scraps of paper. Not a big deal, but it took away from her professional image.
- Does your mobile phone project a tech-savvy image, or are you using a relic from a decade or two back?

Keep it simple. If you are interviewing, don't cart a whole bunch of stuff along with you. Simply carrying a portfolio makes it look as if you belong, like an employee coming from another office rather than a tourist with a day's supplies.

Grooming and Hygiene

Even some of your best friends may not tell you if you have grooming issues. We think it should go without saying that proper grooming is a necessity, but our experience tells us that it still needs a mention. Bad breath, body odor, and other basics can be subtle (or not-so-subtle) turnoffs that you're not even aware of. Don't let your great work and experience be overshadowed by these things, which can (usually) be easily fixed. Ask someone who will be completely honest with you about these issues. And pay attention to your teeth. At the least, brush before any meeting to avoid showing off your lunch leftovers. If you have visibly damaged or misaligned teeth, or if you have chronic halitosis, it might be worth consulting with a dentist.

Office (Cubicle) Space

What does your cube or office look like? If it looks as if a bomb just went off, it says something about you. Even if you have a large sign reading "A messy office is the sign of a creative mind!" it is still risky to live like a slob in your workspace. This is even more important if you work in shared workspace.

- If you organize by piles, make sure they're neat.
- If you have a bookcase, arrange it nicely.
- Accessories and photos can be conversation starters, telling something about your interests or culture. Make sure the images are those you want to project.

Car

If you use a car for work, pay attention to its condition. If you had to give your boss a ride in your car tomorrow, would she come away with dog hair on her clothes? Would you have to move hamburger wrappers and handfuls of Cheerios off the seat? Nancy remembers working for her company's general sales manager, who had strong opinions about what cars should look like, especially company cars. As he was walking Nancy to her car after a meeting, he spotted an old car with worn upholstery. He commented, "One of the locals needs a raise." She felt embarrassed as she put her keys into the lock to open that car. She was actually replacing it the next week, but he had made a judgment about her—not fatal, but not helpful. Cars aren't important to her, but they are to some people.

Mei Works on Her Image

Mei really took to heart the idea of shaping her appearance and presence. She realized she was doing it naturally at the restaurant, where she tried to make good eye contact and smile at all of her customers, knowing that if she did it well, her tips would increase. She stood tall and confident, and she made sure her uniform was always clean and pressed and her hair neat. She applied this to her job search.

Mei did some networking at a few companies and got feedback that she looked very young, partly because her hairstyle and clothing looked more like those of a college student than a business professional. One of the companies in her area with frequent HR openings is Acme Corporation. Acme employees frequent the restaurant Mei works at, so Mei did some research. She noticed that while some Acme employees wore business casual and occasional sport coats, many of their coworkers wore suits. If she wanted to interview there, she would have to up her game.

With that information and her other feedback, Mei went to a moderately priced shop and invested in a "conservative casual" outfit for networking and a suit for her interviews. She also went to a beauty consultant and got a good trim on her hair. When she felt she was ready, she asked some of the Acme people if they would help her with informational interviews at their company. She knew from the looks she got when she walked into the office that she had hit the bull's-eye on her look.

With her careful research on the company, the good service she had provided to Acme employees at the restaurant, and the confidence projected by her professional appearance, it's not surprising that the people at Acme became interested in hiring Mei.

ADDITIONAL CONSIDERATIONS

Although many factors about appearance are universal to everyone in the working world, some considerations vary by age group and deserve comment.

Older Workers—Age and Appearance

Older workers bring much wisdom and experience to the workplace, and these traits are increasingly valued by employers. Many people now have to or want to work well into their sixties, seventies, or beyond. They need to make sure they are valued by coworkers and interviewers. In addition to ensuring that skills and knowledge are current, this group needs to project vitality and currency. They need to make sure their appearance reflects the energy and drive they bring to their companies.

- Choose a haircut in a current style that still fits you. One common question we've had from the fifty-plus crowd is, to dye or not to dye? It depends. For some people, a good color job can take years off their appearance. We emphasize "good," because we've all seen "not good." Have it done professionally, or have someone show you how to select a good color and apply it. Very long gray or salt-and-pepper hair looks good on relatively few people—women or men. Keep it short and styled well; pure gray can be dashing if the style is right.
- You may have heard about the "senior slump"—the rounded shoulders baby boomers may have. Practice standing tall. Take yoga or an exercise class to ensure you are standing as tall as you can. None of us needs to look any older than we already are.
- Let's face it—as you get older, you have a few more aches and pains. However, we've heard a recruiter say he lost interest in an otherwise good candidate who groaned and murmured "Oof!" as he sat down in his chair. Don't groan as you sit down or stand up from a chair. Practice springing up with energy as you stand.

Xers and Millennials—Youthful Confidence

In our multigenerational workplaces, twenty- and thirty-somethings also need to pay attention to the image they project to their organizations, including their bosses and bosses' bosses. Although young and energetic, you still want to project an image of maturity and readiness to take on responsibility.

- Even in casual workplaces, dressing too casually can cut chances for moving ahead. Jeans and leggings, frayed cuffs, clothing with holes, and the like may be okay with your peers outside work, but they won't accelerate your career.
- Tattoos and body piercings should be tasteful and not excessive.

Baby boomer bosses expect employees to be effective on the telephone in order to build relationships with customers, convey information, and project a positive image of the company. A recent article in the *Minneapolis Star Tribune* featured a young man who was "completely flabbergasted" when, just four months after he was hired as a commodities trader, he was let go because of his poor phone skills. Texting, tweeting, and blogging do not necessarily develop all the communication skills needed in today's organizations.

Everyday Speech—Your Choice of Language

It's not just appearance and confidence that affect our reputations. How we present ourselves in our everyday speech also contributes to our reputation. Again, whole books are written on this subject, but we include a few suggestions here.

- Speak clearly and at an audible volume, neither too loudly nor too softy. Ask coworkers for their feedback, or practice with a friend. Remember that some meeting areas magnify sound, while others muffle it.
- Pay attention to your tone and cadence. Speaking too fast makes you hard to follow and suggests a lack of thoughtfulness on a subject. Speaking too slowly can make you sound sleepy or confused, or gives the impression that you're talking down to others. Consult books or articles on public speaking for good tips.

- Speak confidently, not tentatively. Use assertive rather than dismissive language. For example:

  Phrases such as "I don't know if this is a good idea, but . . ." or "This might not work, but . . ." don't convey confidence.

  Instead, language such as "Here's an idea that might move us toward a solution. . ." or "I believe I have a solution that might work . . ." or "Building on what John just said . . ." gives you a more confident sound.

  Use "I think" instead of "I feel." In most organizational cultures, saying "I think" is more likely to make you heard.

- Very assertive language can be too aggressive for some organizational cultures. Stating "I have a solution for that" may appear too confident, for example. It's important to get a feel for how things get said and heard by others in order to understand the culture you're in.
- Learn and use good basic grammar. Some people didn't have the advantage of mastering this in school, so feedback from your boss or someone else you trust is important. We are shocked at the number of misuses of grammar in the workplace—using "should of went" instead of "should have gone," for example. It may not be important to you, but poor grammar can be like fingernails on a blackboard for others.
- Be careful of using slang, rough language, or curse words in the workplace. It will keep you from promotions just as surely as sloppy appearance or other bad habits. If you must, become "bilingual," speaking one style of language at work and another outside the office.
- If you are not a native English speaker, make sure you can be easily understood by your peers, superiors, and customers. Get feedback from a trusted friend; if necessary, get a language coach or take a speech class where you can practice and get feedback.

- Let your voice be heard: speak up at every meeting, as early in the meeting as makes sense. Get on the agenda at meetings whenever possible.

NATASHA'S REALIZATION

Natasha has been concerned for some time about her "executive presence." While she knows her appearance is top drawer, she feels she lacks a commanding presence. She thought back and realized something: when she spoke in meetings, people—particularly people at higher levels—didn't pick up on what she said, but when a *man* said the same thing a few minutes later, most of them picked up on it.

She realized that although this might be a typical situation for women in the workforce, there were some things she personally could do differently to work against this cultural challenge.

She brought up this topic with her boss. He gave her some examples of her speech being tentative, using phrases such as "Maybe . . ." or "I don't know if this is a good idea, but . . ." These speech habits were not serving her well at the executive level. In fact, downplaying ownership and introducing ideas in a tentative way diminished what she had to say. She started practicing presence: maintaining eye contact, using active listening techniques, and paying attention to her posture and speech mannerisms. Slowly, Natasha began to get a little more attention when meeting with senior executives. She decided she would continue practicing these changes to make sure they became part of her natural behavior.

TAKE ACTION TO POWER YOUR CAREER

Take care to look your best and present yourself as a confident, well-spoken individual. As is any form of communication, your physical presence—how you look and how you talk—is as much about your comfort level as it is about what you say.

- Get feedback from trusted colleagues and bosses on how you project yourself, and seek ideas for improving how you present yourself.
- Observe other people who make strong positive impressions. Look for specific actions and behaviors that contribute to their presence. Make notes.
- Pay attention to the details of your appearance. One small thing can completely change the impression you create.

SECTION TWO

CULTIVATE STRATEGIC RELATIONSHIPS

CULTIVATE STRATEGIC RELATIONSHIPS

Relationships are all there is. . . . We have to stop pretending we are individuals that can do it alone.

—Meg Wheatley

Imagine: You have put your heart and soul into doing a great job for your organization. You've put in long hours, you've been a great team player, you've received awards and accolades for your work. Then, to your surprise, someone outside the organization gets the job you were hoping for. How could that have happened?

Doing great work and knowing and articulating your value are necessary for your career to advance, but they're not sufficient to maximize your success. People need to know about you. That is, the right people (those who have power and influence over your career opportunities) need to know about you and what you can do for them. Without the help of strategic relationships, your career or business is likely to plateau. But it's never too late to begin cultivating relationships that matter.

Let's revisit the four people you met in section 1. They have been working on their positioning, their brands, and how to talk about their accomplishments. But now they face additional challenges.

NATASHA has continued her successful run in a senior marketing role in her company, and she is making inroads into international marketing. Her boss trusts her marketing expertise and is pleased with her results. However, because Natasha has been focused exclusively on her deliverables, she is not well known by her boss's peers and superiors. Her company is going through a major restructuring, and the senior leadership team is drawing on their succession plan to promote one of three marketing directors to a VP role with some international aspects to it. When Natasha's name comes up, most people in the room say they don't know her well and don't know much about her. Because she lacks a senior network, her promotional chances don't look good at this time.

GEORGE has now been running his own business for six months. It looks like a real consulting firm: he has crafted his value proposition, built a website, articulated his products and services in compelling ways, and even rewritten his LinkedIn profile. So far, however, "build it and they will come" has not been a winning business development strategy. He has worked with a lot of people in former companies, and they like and respect him. But he has been reluctant to leverage these relationships or their goodwill. He hasn't even gone back to his advocate, Lee, who offered assistance. He's realizing he has to do something different if he is to be successful in his business.

MEI interviewed with several companies and landed an HR specialist job at the Acme Corporation. She is now a few years out of school and has been in HR benefit analyst roles with Acme for most of that time. She has put a lot of hours into her job and learned it well, and she gets good feedback from her superiors. She's recently been thinking about looking for another role within HR in order to broaden her experience, but her boss is not well connected, and he certainly hasn't advocated for her. Feeling a little stifled in her job,

Mei starts looking at the internal job postings but doesn't see anything that fits. She's at a loss as to what to do next.

HENRY now has a file full of accomplishments to talk about and a good brand statement, but he still has not landed a new job. As an IT professional, he knows how to use the Internet efficiently and works with a number of job boards. He has sent dozens if not hundreds of applications for both temporary and full-time positions. However, they seem to be going into a black hole. He checks to see if his cell phone is still working. Funds are running low, and Henry is ready to consider a different approach. The first thing he'll do is to get out of his pajamas and out of the house.

As these four stories illustrate, no matter how brilliant you are, how good a job you do, or how compelling your value proposition, your career will not take off if you don't have people on your side to power it. Cultivating authentic, lasting relationships is key to career success and the primary driver of tactful self-promotion.

In this section, we'll shift our focus from who you are to who you know, working on cultivating strategic relationships throughout your career.

Here's what we'll cover in the next four chapters:

Chapter 5: Get Your Mindset Right—It's about Relationships

Building a network is not about just about creating a long list of names. It's about building deep, meaningful, and mutual relationships. This won't happen unless you have adopted a mindset of truly appreciating relationships and the richness other people can bring to your life—and you to theirs—as well as the power they can add to your career. In this chapter, we'll show you the difference the right mindset can make.

CULTIVATE STRATEGIC RELATIONSHIPS

- Get Your Mindset Right - It's about Relationships
- Develop Your Networking Strategy
- Expand Key Relationships
- Maximize Executive Contacts

Chapter 6: Develop Your Networking Strategy

Most of us don't know all the people we want or need to know right now. There are lots of ways to initiate and maintain relationships. It starts with a goal and a plan—who do you need to know, who do you need to know better, which relationships do you need to nurture? In this chapter, we'll give you some suggestions on where to start, how to put a plan together, and how to prioritize your contacts.

Chapter 7: Expand Key Relationships

A network consists of acquaintances (or general contacts), allies, and advocates. It needs new blood or new relationships to remain vital, and it needs nurturing to thrive. But just how do you initiate new relationships? And how do you cultivate those general contacts so they become more than just a pile of business cards—so they become allies and advocates? You need a strategy for cultivating the all-important asset, your advocates. And finally, it is all a waste if you don't stay connected. As your network grows, it becomes more difficult to manage without some sort of plan. We'll sketch such a plan and also share strategies and tips for making sure your relationships last and have influence for years to come.

Chapter 8: Maximize Executive Contacts

Most of us would like to be known by the executives in our organizations or professions, but we don't have much opportunity to interact with them—and when we do get a chance, we're often not prepared! These are moments for which you want to be prepared, ready to speak up in a way that is comfortable. Your immediate boss is also important. Not everyone is blessed with a great boss, but like them or not, bosses have enormous influence on our career prospects in the form of performance appraisals, raises, bonuses, and promotions. Hence, it helps to build a solid relationship with your boss. This is a little different from other relationships, and we'll provide some tips for attending to that relationship.

Overall, this section provides you with practical ideas you can adapt to help you become more comfortable and adept at connecting with others and building the kind of network that will help you accomplish your goals.

CHAPTER 5

GET YOUR MINDSET RIGHT—IT'S ABOUT RELATIONSHIPS

The only way to have a friend is to be one.

—Ralph Waldo Emerson

Relationships and social interaction are essential parts of life. Without them, we don't have a life. Through our relationships, we learn and we grow: they are the context for everything we do. So developing relationships of all sorts is the ultimate opportunity for growth. And not growth as in just business opportunity; we mean growth in terms of personal development.

Most people are surprised by how generous and helpful people are when approached by someone with the right mindset.

Many people abhor the thought of networking and think they're not good at it or that they can't do it. We think this is because they don't have a proper understanding of what networking is or how to comfortably, effectively, and authentically do it. Networking is *not* about stalking someone with a résumé or building a stack of business cards. It's *not* about "selling" yourself to everyone you know—in fact it's not "selling" at all! It's simply about building meaningful, trusting, reciprocal relationships. And we believe that everyone—even introverts—can do this and do it well. Even well enough to begin to enjoy it. In fact, most people are surprised by how generous and helpful people are when approached by someone with the right mindset.

WHY DEVELOP RELATIONSHIPS?

Why would you want to develop relationships that might "cost" you time and energy? Because *network = net worth*! While the quality of your relationships is critically important, quantity is also important. You won't get ahead if few people know who you are and what your value is. Some time ago, a *New York Times* article described research showing that an executive's net worth directly correlated to the size of his or her network. People with bigger networks make more money! This makes sense, because the greater the number of people who know you, the more opportunities you are likely to discover.

Jeffrey Pfeffer, professor of organizational behavior at Stanford, has marshaled evidence in this arena in his book *Power: Why Some People Have It—and Others Don't*. He shows that when it comes to getting promoted, strong relationships and being on good terms with your boss can matter more to career success than performance. Do you need any more reasons to develop your relationship skills? There are hundreds of books—good and bad—about building relationships and networking. It's not our intention to cover the entire topic of relationship building in this section; we'll just cover some of the most common, most feared, and most important areas. If you want to refine your networking skills further, check out the resources listed at the end of this book.

We must point out that not every relationship type we'll talk about in this section is a strategic relationship. Some are just nice, friendly connections. However, when you start out, you don't know which relationships will be strategic and which may introduce you to more strategic people. And all of them have value.

Moreover, developing a relationship is not a selfish act. A good relationship is a reciprocal relationship. Reciprocity is one of the fundamental motivators of human action. So networking isn't a self-serving activity; it's about developing relationships where you might easily give as much as you get, if not more so.

So networking isn't a self-serving activity; it's about developing relationships where you might easily give as much as you get, if not more so.

Giving is beneficial to your mind and body. When you give, you are focused on another's needs. Bonding with others creates not just good feelings but also positive brain chemistry. When you give to another, your brain releases the "love hormone" oxytocin, which has not only a calming effect on your brain but also anti-inflammatory properties.

If giving is good for you, then providing others with the opportunity to help you benefits them as well! In short, authentic, reciprocal relationships benefit both parties. The problem is that most people don't see networking in these terms. They see it as a self-serving attempt to get others to do things for them. If you take that approach, you won't be very effective.

Building relationships is a natural part of life. People have always had networks—they just didn't label them that way. Prior to the computer age, people talked about "connections." Today's network metaphor has an unfortunate tendency to depersonalize relationship building and make it sound like a mechanical system or process. It's neither.

Network should be a noun before it's a verb. In other words, don't wait to build relationships until you have a need for something, as Harvey Mackay says in *Dig Your Well Before You're Thirsty*. The best time to start building a base of relationships is *before* you need help, *before* you are trying to find a new customer, or *before* you're looking for a job. It's much easier to approach someone to ask a favor if you have already built a relationship. Building relationships is a way of life—a way in which many people effectively manage their careers and their lives—and it could and should be yours.

YOU'RE KNOWN BY THE COMPANY YOU KEEP

Relationships also matter because the people you spend time with shape who you are and who you become. Behavior and beliefs are contagious: you easily "catch" your friends' emotional states, imitate their actions, and absorb their values as your own. What we see others doing is a huge driver of our own behavior. As much as we like to think of ourselves as rugged individualists, the fact is, we are designed to be copycats. In social science this tendency is called "social proof." We are influenced by others far more than we realize. If you're driving down the interstate and everyone passes you going a lot faster, you're likely to speed up. If you come across a group of people looking up at the sky, it will be hard for you not to do the same. Social proof drives so much of our behavior.

So, if your friends are the types who get stuff done, chances are you'll be that way too. The fastest way to change yourself is to hang out with people who are already the way you want to be. Conversely, hanging out with the wrong people can be disastrous to your career.

Our purpose for encouraging networking here is to help you become more visible to more people and for other people to become more visible to you. However, we sincerely hope that as you get more comfortable with building a network, you will value relationships and appreciate the enjoyment and education of connecting with a variety of different people.

TYPICAL BARRIERS

Before you start building, you have to understand what's standing in your way. Here are a few common beliefs that block people from building strategic relationships.

WHAT'S IN YOUR WAY?	MAY BE TRUE FOR ME	NOT TRUE FOR ME
1. I don't really know that many people.		
2. Why would people help me, anyway?		
3. I don't feel I know anyone well connected.		
4. The last time I talked to this person, I was looking for a job, and now I need to ask for something again . . . It seems I'm always asking for help.		
5. I don't know what to say during a networking conversation.		
6. I don't know if I have that much to offer other people.		
7. I'm not good at making small talk with people I don't know well.		
8. I don't have a good reason to call . . . I don't know why I'm doing it.		
9. Other people are really busy, and I don't want to be a bother.		
10. I was raised not to ask for help.		
11. I'm busy—I don't have time to invest in building relationships.		
12. The last time I tried reaching out to someone, the person was not helpful.		
13. I don't need other people.		

Anywhere you marked "May be true for me" could be a barrier. We all have them. The first step in overcoming your barriers is to become aware of them. Just pay attention to your thought processes, and you'll begin to see what's keeping you from cultivating relationships. You'll find ways to address these areas in this chapter and throughout the rest of this book. We'll help you not only get over these barriers but also get excited about networking!

Let's briefly revisit Henry, our job seeker. After months of frustration, he figured out what was in his way. He didn't know what to say during a networking meeting, and he wasn't sure why he was calling potential connections. To develop a sense of purpose in his networking, he picked a small number of people with whom he wanted deeper connections and did some research, learning what their interests and needs were. Rather than worrying about his own performance and how each conversation might move his job search forward, Henry found that taking a genuine interest in others allowed him to focus on relationship building for the long term. He even started enjoying himself (which meant that others also enjoyed connecting with him).

CULTIVATING A RELATIONSHIP ATTITUDE

Creating a more positive personal attitude about developing relationships and networking can make it much easier to approach other people. Here are a few strategies to try.

Reframe Networking as Research—Not Selling!

Many people hate the idea of networking because they think of it as selling—and the worst kind of selling. However, we suggest approaching it as research, because that's exactly what it is. When you connect with people, you are usually trying to find something out—for example, information on different companies, advice on your career, names of other people who may be able to help you. And most people are happy to help you with research.

Be Authentic

Being Authentic is one of the core principles of this book. It may take you out of your comfort zone at times, but you still have to be yourself—you have to build relationships in a way that is authentically you, not something you read in a book (even this book!). Take these ideas and adapt them to work well for you. This leads to rich, lasting relationships that are reciprocal and mutually beneficial.

George, our entrepreneur, is a very personable guy who is well liked by his former coworkers. He naturally connects with everyone. When you're out with George, no matter where you are, several people are bound to come up to him just to say hello. George's authenticity and natural charm have built him a strong network. But if truth be told, he gives as much to his network as he gets. Now he has to begin tapping them for help in his research to find customers.

Use Your Listening Skills

Dale Carnegie, author of the classic book *How to Win Friends and Influence People,* never goes out of style. Developing a genuine interest in others' interests and needs and focusing on what they say are essential tools for building relationships. You can learn a lot about someone by actively listening to them rather than thinking of your reply while they are still talking. You can learn about their strongest interests, their most important experiences, and how they relate to the world—all important information that could help you communicate with them very effectively.

Developing a genuine interest in others' interests and needs and focusing on what they say are essential tools for building relationships.

If you aren't as good a listener as you should be, work on developing these skills. When listening to someone, focus your attention to the point that when he or she is finished, you could repeat back the essence of what was said to you.

Listening isn't difficult. It just takes effort and focus: effort to stop making judgments, and focus to stay on the other person's agenda instead of getting lost in your own thoughts.

Add Value and Give to Others

While we often call on our networks when we need something, it is still essential to focus on other people and their needs before your own. Other people need to get value out of the relationship as well. Find out what others think is important. Think about how *you* might be of use to *them*. Knowing what you might offer them can make networking more palatable if you find networking distasteful. You're not striving for exact reciprocity in every single meeting, but over time you should give as much as you get.

Some people are intimidated by the idea of giving to others. They assume they don't have anything to give, particularly to people in much more senior roles. Here are a few suggestions to get you started:

- Ask what you could do to help them. Even if you don't think there is any possible way you could help them, you might be surprised!
- Listen to their needs. You may be able to help them with connections or resources, even with seemingly unrelated matters such as their kids' applications to soccer camp or where to find a good tennis coach or trainer. Simply listening may make them feel valued.
- Pass along copies of or links to articles of interest to them.
- Ask them what kind of business referrals they'd like to get for *their* business.

Be Willing to Ask for Help

Like George, many people have a strong and wide network of relationships with people who like them. They have lots of great conversations. They have built up a great deal of goodwill over the years.

However, they have a hard time making the ask; they seem to think that people should already know what they need. But people appreciate being *asked*, and they need to know exactly what it is that you need from them.

Stay Connected

Adopting a mindset of relationship building means you don't just jump from one person to the next. You need to stay in touch in a way that fits the type of relationship. Some connections are casual, so an e-mail or holiday card once a year is an appropriate vehicle for staying in touch. For others, such as your advocates, you need to connect far more frequently.

MARTHA'S SUCCESS

Martha, a young freelance writer and journalist and acquaintance who came to Nancy for help, perhaps best illustrates adopting a new mindset about building a network. She was tired of freelance work and wanted to break into the world of corporate communications, but she was not having any luck. Nancy tried coaching her on how to network . . . no change. Tried again . . . no change. Finally, one day, a lightbulb seemed to go on in Martha's eyes. She got it! Within a few months, Martha had built a small but powerful network of people in her field and landed the type of job she wanted in an organization she was happy with. What happened?

Over a glass of wine with Nancy two years later, Martha shared the key to her changed mindset. What had been holding her back? Previously, she had *hated* what she thought networking was all about: she didn't want to be in a position of needing something and asking people for things. She thought she was being an opportunist, a leech, a taker, a self-promoter—all of which made her cringe. Suddenly, she started seeing it differently: as a reporter, she called people every day and asked them questions, looking for information or advice. She began to see networking as simply an extension of this. Soon she had no problem calling people and asking, "Can we meet for coffee?"

What changed? According to Martha,

1. She thinks of networking as making new friends, rather than "finding someone I could get something from." She now anticipates it with joy rather than dread.

2. She thinks in terms of developing long-term relationships as opposed to collecting a pile of business cards.

3. She realizes she has something to offer. It's a two-way street, and she has a wealth of experience that allows her to do things *for* others instead of just taking *from* them.

Martha got more involved in a professional association and soon ended up chairing an awards committee. How did she get this job done? She pulled together a committee of high-level people she had met through networking, focusing on those who enjoyed committee work and strengthening their own network relationships. She was able to get the expertise she needed and give others a chance to expand their networks as well.

In reality, not all stories go flawlessly. Martha now has a young child and is in a new, more stressful job. In the last few years, she has not worked at keeping her network up. She misses it. She now feels that networking makes a person well-rounded. As she says, "We're not automatons; we're social beings." After her evening with Nancy, she was determined to be more diligent about keeping her network alive and growing. She's working on our Networking Plan for a Year guide, which you can find on our website.

Why do you think this approach worked for Martha? First of all, she changed her mindset: how you think about networking influences how you carry it out. If you treat it as just a technique you read about but don't really want to do, people will see through it. People need to see you are authentically interested in meeting them and learning more about their lives and goals. Martha sincerely changed her mindset from wanting help in finding her next job to wanting to develop long-term relationships.

In the true spirit of reciprocal relationships, Martha recently gave Nancy an opportunity to post a guest blog on her company's website. This brought useful information to Martha's company and helped Nancy market her business as well.

GEORGE, MEI, AND NATASHA SHIFT THEIR MINDSETS

Building relationships is a skill for career survival and life. And as Martha's case demonstrates, it can be learned. In very few careers are technical skills more important than relationship skills, and even then, the person who has both is way ahead of the competition. Ask recruiters, and they will tell you that interpersonal skills are as important, if not *more* important, than technical skills when they evaluate candidates. While a networking meeting may be only a one-time thing, networking is not an event or a series of events. It's a priceless opportunity to practice how you manage your career and your life.

Interpersonal skills are as important, if not ***more*** *important, than technical skills.*

George finally began to realize he had a wealth of people who liked and respected him, but he was not tapping into this resource effectively. When he went through the checklist about barriers, he saw he was not comfortable asking for help. He talked with his friend Lee and realized he had been hoping the people in his network would just come forward to help. However, he wasn't clearly telling them what he needed and how they could help him in his research to find potential customers. Once he got clear on this, he began to feel more comfortable setting up meetings with people he knew.

Mei's issuc was a little different: she knew her boss was not a strong player in the organization, and she couldn't count on him to help her connect within the company. However, she didn't want to go around him and risk the political fallout. Once she wrapped her mind around the fact that networking was mostly research, she realized that learning more about the company and her profession was good not only for her but also for the company. She started setting up breakfast and lunch meetings with other benefits specialists around town to learn more about her specialty, and she brought that knowledge back to her department. All while expanding her network!

Natasha knew she needed to make connections at more senior levels, but she felt a bit intimidated. So she reached out to someone who was a terrific networker, well connected at the top, and asked for advice. That person suggested that Natasha start with her boss and ask for help. Natasha was so focused on having to prove herself that she hadn't even thought of asking her boss for help. She set up a meeting with him for the next week.

TAKE ACTION TO POWER YOUR CAREER

Most of us could benefit from a tune-up on our networking skills. Adopting a constructive mindset is generally a first step.

- Go through the checklist at the beginning of this chapter and revisit the two or three statements that represent your biggest barriers to networking. What are some of the reasons for this? What could you do to get over these hurdles? What are your fears about networking?
- Pay attention during interactions to ensure you're taking time to listen to and show genuine interest in the people around you.
- Articulate what you have to offer people, so you always feel you're in a position to give as well as receive.

CHAPTER 6

DEVELOP YOUR NETWORKING STRATEGY

You can make more friends in two months by becoming interested in other people than you can in two years by trying to get other people interested in you.

—Dale Carnegie

After working on branding and positioning themselves, Natasha, Mei, George, and Henry know much more about themselves and their value propositions, and they are much better prepared to share them. However, knowing how to talk about themselves is just the first step. Each needs more connections, but each has different priorities: Natasha needs to get known more broadly by upper-level people in her organization and perhaps in her profession. Mei needs to become better known in the human resources profession and by managers in her own company. George needs to meet people in the organizations that might engage his services. And Henry needs to learn who's doing what in the IT world and which companies would be a good fit for him.

Building a network of relationships starts with determining your goals. In which areas do you want to expand? What do you want to learn? What kinds of people do you want or need to get to know? For example, Mei will probably make it a priority to meet people who work or have worked in HR departments. By getting to know more HR people, she can learn more about how other companies perform HR work, where she might fit into another HR department, who the decision makers are, and who is likely to hire someone with her background.

WHO SHOULD BE IN YOUR NETWORK?

Everyone interested in their career ought to build a broad and diverse network in

- their organization,
- their profession,
- their industry, and
- their communities and personal lives.

You also ought to have different types of relationships in your network:

- ***Acquaintances***—These general contacts are people who know you by name, and you know their names as well. They may be employees at your firm, connections on LinkedIn, friends of friends, members of your church, parents of your kids' friends. They have had some personal experience with you but have only a little knowledge about you. They probably don't know enough about you to give a reference, but they might be willing to do something for you—introduce you to someone else, pass your résumé forward, and so on—if you ask.
- ***Allies***—These are people with whom you share some kind of common ground. They may be people you have worked with, volunteered with, or know through a book club or golf. They probably are familiar with at least some of your

talents, skills, and aspirations. Allies can speak to your character, strengths, and results because they have had some interaction with you.

- ***Advocates***—These are people who know you very well and believe in you. They are your walking ambassadors. In *The 20-Minute Networking Meeting*, Marcia Ballinger and Nathan Perez call them your "evangelists." They are willing to put their good names on the line to speak on your behalf. They will pick up the phone and make a call for you—in fact, they may do it without your even asking!

Building Your Strategy

Now that you have an idea of who should be in your network, outline a strategy to build up your network of meaningful relationships:

1. **Identify who is in your network now.**

   Take a few minutes and jot down at least ten to twenty names in each of the above categories: Acquaintances, Allies, and Advocates. To build your list, it may be helpful to think in categories: relatives, neighbors, and church acquaintances; work contacts (past and present bosses, coworkers, and direct reports); key people in your current organization; school connections (teachers and classmates, alumni associations), volunteer organizations, bowling league; vendors and customers; trade, industry, or professional organizations; search firms; parents of your children's friends, soccer parents, and so on.

   - Always keep a notepad—electronic or paper—handy, because once you start this process, you'll think of random people while you're running an errand or waiting in the dentist's office.
   - Add as many people as you can think of to your list, including every name that comes to mind. Don't worry about how long it's been since you last spoke to these peo-

ple or how long ago you knew them. Don't worry that they do not live in your city. They may be dormant, but they still may be able to help you. And don't screen out anyone by assuming they don't know very many people or may not remember you.

Most people who have been working for a few years should be able to come up with at least two hundred names already in their networks. If you've been working for a long time, it should be quite easy to come up with three or four hundred—or more. The majority will be acquaintances or general contacts; you will probably have only a few advocates at this point.

BUILDING YOUR CONTACT DATABASE

- You can use a commercial contact management system, but many people use a spreadsheet or Word table for their purposes.
- Create a database you can add to and that is sortable so you can easily find people in it.
- Think through how you will be using this list before setting it up. For example, people going into business for themselves may want to categorize different types of contacts (e.g., customers, potential customers, referral sources). People who plan on staying in their current organizations may want to categorize the list into search firms, people in their profession, former coworkers and bosses, and people in organizations where they may want to work. This can be done at a later date, but it's easier to build the structure early.
- Build in helpful fields: Name (last and first—set up so it can be sorted), Contact Information, Last Date of Contact, Date for Next Contact, and Notes (including where you got the name, the names the contact gave you, other things of interest).
- When you meet new people or get names from someone, add their information to the list immediately (after sending them a follow-up note and inviting them to connect on LinkedIn!).
- Review the list regularly (monthly or at least quarterly) to identify people you should be contacting in the next period of time.

Now put this new, precious list into a contact database. You'll be using this for a long time, and it will become more valuable to you over time, so make the effort now to set up a system that will work for the long term.

2. Clarify your goals.

Before you start networking, get clear about why you want to build a network. What kind of information will you be seeking? Are you researching a certain topic or industry? Do you want to make a move within your organization? Do you want to change organizations? Are you starting a business and looking for potential customers? Are you out of work and looking for employment? Are you simply trying to meet new people in your community? Are you looking for people who share hobbies and interests? Your answers to these questions should be a guide to setting goals for relationships you want to develop or strengthen. Equally important, your goals should help you develop the questions you want to ask people.

3. Assess the strength of your current network.

A vibrant network will broaden opportunities. Before you prioritize and plan your actions, assess your current network to see how large, deep, and diverse it is.

How large is your network? While quality of relationships is definitely critical, quality and quantity are not an either/or situation: you need both. This is a good time to mention LinkedIn (and Facebook): If you've been careful about accepting invitations to connect on LinkedIn, most of your connections should be part of your network. If you've never met some connections face to face, they may not really be part of your network yet.

How deep are your relationships? How well do you know the people in your network? Do you find you have lots of general contacts but not so many allies and advocates? How often do they hear from you? Mostly just when you need something? Or do you reach out from time to time with nice gestures? Again, we think many of your LinkedIn connections are not deep—they would go into your acquaintance bucket at best.

How diverse is your network? As you look at the names on your list, are they all from the same corner of your life? College friends? Coworkers? Soccer parents? Church friends? All the same age, race, and gender? Do you have people who represent your current organization, profession, industry, and community?

If you find your network is insufficiently large, deep, or diverse, don't worry—the next chapter will help you expand your relationships.

4. Prioritize your network list.

You can't talk with everybody all at once. You need to start somewhere. So take some time to prioritize your list of contacts. Here's a way to get started.

From your current network: After the assessment you did in step 3, you should have a good idea of your network's strengths. Allies and advocates pack the most punch in your network, so your first goal is to find more of them. You probably have a few of these potential resources in your network already, and they're often a good place to start because you've already connected—think of it as a chance to catch up rather than make a request.

- Look at your advocates and allies or people who are very close to being advocates or allies. Select ten to nurture and strengthen in the next year.
- Select at least ten allies or acquaintances with whom you want to deepen your relationship over the next year.

People with whom you'd like to connect: These are people you don't yet know and who don't know you at this point. In fact, you may not be able to name specific people—perhaps you just have some ideas about the type of people you'd like to know. These are people you will want to bring into your network.

If you are early in your career, like Mei, and don't have a clear career niche, your list might include:

- Friends of your parents who have interesting careers or are in interesting organizations.
- An executive in your company who might be willing to talk with you, even if this isn't the company you want to spend your career in.
- A few people in your major who graduated with you or ahead of you. What are they doing now, and how is it working for them? What career wisdom or questions do they have now?
- Employees of organizations for which you might like to work, even if you're not clear on what you'd want to do there.
- A career coach who can help you think about what you are really good at and what you want to do.
- Your current boss. While it's easy to overlook your current boss, be sure to ask for his or her suggestions and support when building a network. Ask how he or she built a network, whom he or she would suggest you get to know, and what organizations you should join. Depending on the situation, you may want to ask for an introduction or two when you need it.
- Advocates. Your advocates can be a great referral source to people who might be worth meeting. Ask them.

If you are further along in your career, and in marketing, like Natasha, you may include:

- The chief marketing officer in your organization and his or her counterparts at two of the large companies in your area, especially those known for cutting-edge work.
- The head of a trusted vendor that works with your company.
- One or two executives in your own organization, especially in areas you are interested in learning about or working in someday.
- Recruiters at one or two search firms or key search people in your market.
- A marketing professional who is considered one of the best, or one who is considered a "hot" up-and-comer.
- A reporter at the local newspaper who reports on business.
- The president of the local chapter of a professional or industry association, especially if he or she seems to be respected by many.
- A thought leader in your profession. (See chapter 12 for more on thought leaders.)
- And of course, your boss can a good source of help (although not all are).

Natasha needed more senior-level visibility in her own organization, so she put her boss and the heads of her company's international and sales departments at the top of her list. She also decided to make an appointment with the head of a local advertising agency.

At the beginning of this process, you don't have to be specific about all ten slots on the wish-to-connect list. Leave some room for serendipity to help you out. You may run into a great new contact at an event, at happy hour, or even in line at the grocery store.

5. Create a plan for each of the major types of connections.

How will you find time to connect with people you already know as well as to meet new people? This can be challenging for people working full-time. However, if you set goals and plan ahead, it's doable for virtually everyone. Look at your prioritized list of connections. Pick one ally with the potential to become an advocate. Set a deadline by which you will reach out to that person—by the end of the day, by the end of the week—and put it on your calendar or task list. Choose a contact from your acquaintances list and set a deadline by which you will reach out, perhaps by sending a relevant article or inquiring about an upcoming event in your field. Look at your list of advocates and make note of when you'll likely meet next; come up with a question about a topic of shared interest to ask when you get together.

When you meet one deadline, set a new deadline for another name in the same category. Or if planning ahead works for you, set regular deadlines for the next several months. Reaching out takes only a few minutes; most people find that the biggest obstacle is making time to do it. However, once you have gotten into the habit, keeping up contact not only takes less effort but also rewards you with interesting conversations and improved relationships. Chapter 7 will give you a wealth of additional tactics and tips for how to go about it.

6. Research the people you'd like to meet.

It's much easier to contact and connect with someone if you know something about them and their organization. What are their interests, at work and in their free time? There might be a very natural link to something you are interested in. Googling people, checking LinkedIn, reading their organization's website, and asking mutual acquaintances can help you gather information on people you don't know.

One excellent resource is Sam Richter's book *Take the Cold Out of Cold Calling*. Don't let the title throw you off. It's really about how to research people and find ways to warm up a connection, so you're never in the position of making a cold call. Sam even suggests using what you found in your research when you meet the person by saying something such as, "I did some research on the Internet/LinkedIn, and I see you are very active in______________. How did you get into that?" We'll provide some additional ways to initiate relationships in the next chapters.

GEORGE AND HENRY MAKE PLANS

Now let's see what George and Henry did with their networking plans.

George is clear on why he was building his network: he wants business, and he needs introductions to people who could hire him to do work. After working on his positioning statement and his value proposition, he now understands what type of companies need him and could make best use of his skills. So he makes a list of target organizations and does some research into the key people in these organizations.

Next, George starts listing his contacts. Like most people, he finds that his list is much longer than he expected. He had forgotten about all the people who had left his prior employers and now were in new and different organizations, often with promotions to decision-making positions. Many of these people had known him and his work well. George realizes that now that he's clear on his value proposition, he feels comfortable contacting many of them. He just needs to find the path from those he knows to those he wants to do business with. He chooses a few people on his contact list with whom he is most familiar, gets a cup of coffee, and sends out a few e-mails.

Henry's challenge is a little different. He doesn't have a long list of contacts—he had been a bit of a loner in his prior organization. (Oh! how he wishes it had not been so!) However, his list does include a small, close-knit group of former coworkers and a few former supervisors and project leads. He also has professors from his school, with whom he has had little contact. Because he had been on a task force to select a new software vendor, he also has names in a few vendor organizations.

For his goal, Henry notes the names of a few companies that might need talent such as his and that he might like to work for. He plans to call two of his contacts in the next few days to talk about what he does and find out if they know anything about the companies he listed or if they have ideas for other companies. He's beginning to feel that this just might work!

TAKE ACTION TO POWER YOUR CAREER

Your networking will go more smoothly if you have a plan. A shotgun strategy is ineffective and inefficient. So take time to think through your approach.

- Clarify your goal for building your network, and revisit your goal before each e-mail and phone contact.
- Make a list of everyone you know, categorize them, and set priorities for which acquaintances, allies, and advocates you want to focus on over the next year.
- Think about new people you'd like to add to your network (or at least the roles they might be in).
- Look at your calendar. How and when will you carve out some time each day or week to work on your relationships?

CHAPTER 7

EXPAND KEY RELATIONSHIPS

To get a step up in the world, you could use a ladder, or you could use your connections. I prefer the latter.

—Jarod Kintz

Natasha, Mei, George, and Henry have a variety of networking challenges: Natasha needs to develop advocates in her company, Mei needs to develop contacts in her targeted companies, George needs introductions to potential customers, and Henry needs people who can help him find the right jobs in the right types of companies. In this chapter, we'll develop strategies for addressing their different needs.

SET A NETWORKING GOAL

For some people, the hardest part of building a network of connections is reaching out to new people. For others, it's knowing what to say after they've connected or how to strengthen relationships with the people they already know. All of these steps are easier when you have clarified your goals and prepared some ideas of what to talk about.

Nancy once worked with a CEO who had just been let go by the board of directors of his company. He was devastated and worried about what to do. After he polished up his résumé, he acknowledged he had to build a network. But behind closed doors, he finally admitted, "I know I have to call people, but what do I say after they answer the phone and say hello?" Nancy helped him come up with a few opening statements and good questions he could use. The opener was, "Hi. I've had my head full-bore down in XYZ Corporation for fifteen years. I'm out now, trying to learn what's going on in the Twin Cities outside of XYZ. Would you have a few minutes to talk?" (Or, "Would you have time for a cup of coffee?") They practiced it before he began making calls.

At the next meeting with Nancy, he said it worked every time—people were open to talking, and he was expanding meaningful connections. There are several lessons in his experience:

- If you dread reaching out to other people, know that you are not alone—even successful executives are sometimes uncertain about how to approach other people, or they haven't developed their skills or comfort in this area.
- Know what you want from each conversation *before* you pick up the phone.
- Have a few questions or conversation openers that work in your situation (also see chapter 9 on Working the Room). Practice them so they are your own and you can say them confidently.

CONNECT WITH NEW PEOPLE

To build your network of acquaintances, just start talking with people (and listening to them!). Like the CEO we just mentioned, you need to start contacting people. Getting started is easier said than done, but you'll find that connecting is quite easy—and even enjoyable—after you've made the first phone calls. But you have to create that initial momentum!

Remember that a networking call is an authentic, sincere, confident conversation involving shared interests and an information exchange (including getting additional names). The goal for any networking conversation is to deepen the relationship, gain and share information, and provide value to the other person.

The goal for any networking conversation is to deepen the relationship, gain and share information, and provide value to the other person.

Getting Started

Using LinkedIn and other resources (such as professional organizations), find one of your connections who can introduce you to someone you'd like to meet. After the person you know agrees to make the introduction, plan an approach to the new connection. Think through your approach in the context of your larger networking goal. For example, if your broader goal is to find a new job, the goal of a specific phone call may be to gather industry information, to find a contact in one of your target organizations, or to get an introduction to a potential hiring manager. If your broader goal is to become better known in your profession, the goal of a specific phone call may be to ask for an introduction to a thought leader in your profession.

Your connection may be willing to call and make an introduction, but usually an e-mail can provide your connection with enough information to introduce you to the new contact. Write an e-mail about why you want to meet the third person, and send it along with a cover note to your contact so he or she can forward your request.

PHONE OR E-MAIL?

Either will work, depending on your comfort level. Many people prefer some advance knowledge about what you would like to discuss, so an e-mail explaining your goal lets them think about it before they answer your phone call.

You don't know what this new person prefers, so use what you're most comfortable with. What matters is that you reach out, not *how* you reach out. Introverts often prefer to start with e-mail because it lets them plan what they want to say and make changes before they send it. If you use e-mail, we recommend following up with a phone call.

Texting is not okay in this situation nor in most networking conversations.

Here is an example of an e-mail our consultant, George, might send to get an introduction to someone he wants to meet:

> *Dear Mike:*
>
> *When I started my business, you kindly offered to help me. I'd like to ask for your help now. When we worked together, you mentioned that you had experience working with a vendor called MSP and Associates. I want to connect with someone there, as I'm doing research on the __________industry. Don't worry—I won't try to sell them anything or ask for business from them. I just have some questions. Do you have a name and contact information, and would you be willing to make an introduction via e-mail?*
>
> *Thanks in advance,*
>
> *George*

Here is an example of an e-mail Henry might send to his acquaintance Jules to request an introduction to Sarah, someone he'd like to meet:

> *Dear Jules:*
>
> *I noticed in LinkedIn that you are friends with Sarah Meyers. I would very much like to connect with her, and I'm hoping you would be comfortable making an introduction. She seems to be quite an expert in ____________, an area in which I am trying to build some expertise of my own. I'd love to get her advice about how I might become more knowledgeable. If you are willing, would you kindly forward this note to her and perhaps copy me? And then I will take it from there.*
>
> *Thanks for your help and support, Jules.*
>
> *Sincerely,*
>
> *Henry*

Connecting with a Stranger

If you don't know someone who can introduce you to a new contact, get the contact's e-mail address and phone number. Send an e-mail, followed by a phone call. If you can't find the e-mail address, try using an InMail message on LinkedIn.

Here are a few examples of e-mail messages you can tailor to your own style and needs:

> *Hello, Anne-*
>
> *Your name keeps coming up as I meet with people in the Twin Cities. You are very well connected and have a great reputation as an expert in employee benefits, especially those related to "best places to work." Specifically, John Jones mentioned your name when I met with him last week. I'm trying to expand my knowledge of HR and benefits. Would you be willing to have a cup of coffee in the next few*

months to share some information and answer a few of my questions? I am happy to work with your assistant to get this scheduled.

Thank you,

Mei Johnson

(Notice that Mei suggested a time frame of two months. People will much more readily agree to meet with you sometime in the future, rather than in the next week, when they feel they're too busy.)

George might follow up on a conference presentation with:

Dear Mr. Johnson,

I just attended the speech you gave at ______________ and was impressed with your knowledge of ______________. You were so effective at making seemingly dry information exciting, complex, yet easy to understand. I work for XYZ Company in this same field, and I wonder if you'd be willing to meet with me to help me better understand how you apply ___________ in your company. If you'll send me some times, I'll come to a place convenient to you.

Thank you,

George Harrison

And Henry might use something such as:

Dear Ms. Smith,

I saw on LinkedIn that you have worked for XYZ Inc. and have experience in ___________. I am currently striving to increase my knowledge of________________, and it appears you would be an excellent resource, should you be so gracious as to agree to a meeting. In particular I am interested in exploring________________ and ________________________. Would you be willing to have a cup of coffee sometime in the next month, and after that, perhaps we can link?

Thank you in advance,

Henry Jones

When you call someone to request a meeting in the future, they may say, "I have time right now. How can I help you?" If you're lucky enough to get them at a good time, be prepared! Once you start these phone calls, you want to be ready with your questions in case you get the opportunity to talk on the spot with someone.

Learn to Be an Effective Conversationalist

We often hear people say they are hesitant about networking because they are uncomfortable making small talk—that is, conversing about something not task-related. To build a network, you may have to focus on building conversational skills.

Do your research so you know a little about the organization and the person you'll meet. As Marcia Ballinger and Nathan Perez say in their book, don't ask questions about things you could have found by doing some research on LinkedIn or the Internet.

To build a network, you may have to focus on building conversational skills.

Start the conversation by mentioning something the person is interested in or by complimenting the person on something you have observed about him or her or the organization. Your conversation starters should be focused on the other person, and of course, they should be appropriate and respectful. And be sincere; don't overdo it.

The importance of a conversation starter hit home recently when we were interviewing a successful CEO for a project we were doing. Prior to meeting him, we checked his LinkedIn profile, which included a unique, very casual picture. When he walked in the room, dressed in shorts, we said, "You look just like you do in your LinkedIn picture!" This gave him the opening to talk about his second business, a nonprofit that is his passion, and he did so at some length. The connection was immediate.

Take some cues from artifacts in a person's workspace. If you meet the new contact at his or her workplace, notice something in the reception area or in the person's office and comment on it. A golf trophy, a family picture, an award of some sort, artwork—ask about it and, if appropriate, compliment the person on it. The first part of the conversation is about building rapport—and it's about the other person more than about you.

Ask open-ended questions, those that start with *what* or *how*. This requires the other person to reply with more than a one-word answer. Prepare a list of good questions in advance, keeping your goals in mind. People make judgments about you based on the types of questions you ask. (We list some conversation-starting questions in the Work the Room section of chapter 9.) Listen to the answers so you can ask good follow-up questions. Be sure to include a question about what you can do for him or her.

Know how to close a conversation. Be careful to not exceed the time you scheduled for the appointment. If you go over, make sure it's because the other person suggested it, not because you continued past the allotted time. When you're approaching the final minutes, you can say, "I'm conscious of your time—we set this up for thirty minutes, and we're just about there. I have one more question I'd like to ask, and then I'd like to find out if there is anything I can do for you."

Closing comments might include, "Thank you so much for your time and for sharing your wisdom. I'd like to stay in touch with you, if you don't mind. May I e-mail you if I have any questions on this subject?" or, "I now see why people mention your name when the subject of __________ comes up. Your knowledge is impressive, and

I sincerely appreciate your sharing it with me. May I send you an invitation to connect on LinkedIn?"

You can use these tips as starting points to craft your own authentic questions, tailoring them to your needs and to the person you're meeting. The resources section at the end of this book contains even more helpful guidance for networking meetings. *The 20-Minute Networking Meeting* by Marcia Ballinger and Nathan Perez is particularly helpful in this regard.

Additional Ideas and Tips

Every field has its own networking opportunities, but we have used each of the following tips to reach out and add new people to our networks. Pick one and give it a try:

- Reach out, extend your hand, and talk to those ahead of or behind you in lines, or next to you in airline seats. In his book, Harvey Mackay has a funny story about not talking with his seatmate on a flight, only to realize as they were landing—too late—that the person he had been avoiding was Diane Sawyer.
- Attend at least one in-person networking event each month (and apply our suggestions for working the room in chapter 9)
- At the end of every networking meeting or conversation, ask whom else you should be talking to. That way, you'll have even more names of people who might be helpful in your network. Ask how your contact knows the third person, and if he or she will introduce you or if you can use his or her name when you contact the person.
- Always send thank-you notes after meetings. Also send notes of appreciation when someone goes out of the way to help you or provides you with exceptional service. Better yet, if appropriate, send word to that person's boss, specifying what you valued.

- Take calls from search firms and employment agencies—you may not be interested in a particular opportunity, but this is a network contact who may be helpful in the future. Add the recruiter's name and contact information to your database. Offer to refer some people who fit the recruiter's needs (and then follow up and *do* it!). Follow up with a thank-you e-mail and send your résumé, in the event you could be useful to the recruiter in the future.
- Join at least one professional or industry organization and get involved in it for a year. This will make it easy to broaden and deepen your network, and it will help you do the rest of the work we suggest in this section. Attend meetings—you don't have to attend every month, but the more you go, the more relationships you'll develop, and the better the quality. Consider joining a task force or committee that will give you more access to people you want to get to know. It can be easier to attend meetings when you are more involved.
- Write e-mails to authors of articles in newspapers, magazines, or websites—show your interest and ask questions. At the end of most articles, you can find the writer's name and contact information. It is surprising how few people take the time to write a note and how willing the writer might be to respond.

We hope these are helpful ideas for you—however, good ideas and LinkedIn connections do not build a network. You need to set goals, take action, follow up, and measure your results. Make it a goal to meet *at least* one new person a month with whom you can build a long-term relationship.

DEEPENING RELATIONSHIPS WITH PEOPLE YOU KNOW

As important as it is to expand your network, it is equally important to stay in touch and deepen relationships with people already in it. These don't have to be formal meetings—sometimes just quick e-mails or voicemail messages letting them know you were thinking of them is enough, without requiring them to do anything.

Turning Acquaintances into Allies

Start with the goal of deepening your relationship with someone you might know only by name or someone you haven't seen in a while. Pick someone you worked with briefly or connected with on LinkedIn and propose a get-together. Here are a few e-mail examples you can adapt to fit your situation:

- *I just read in the paper that your company was cited as one of the best places to work in our area. Congratulations to you—it must make your job more fun! I'd love to learn more about what your organization does to earn that recognition. Would you have a chance to talk or have a cup of coffee?*
- *I thought about you last week when I stopped in to_____ restaurant for lunch. I remembered a great lunch you and I had there when we were working on the XYZ project. That was a wonderful time in our careers—we did good work together. Would you be open to a cup of coffee to catch up and stay connected?*
- *I just read that your company landed a huge project with__________. Congratulations! I know you have been targeting this business for a long time. There must be some celebrating going on! When you're done celebrating, would you be open for a cup of coffee sometime?*
- *I noticed on LinkedIn that you have a new company and bigger title. Congratulations! I'd love to stay connected and to hear more about your new company. Once you are settled, would you be open to a cup of coffee? We can schedule something a few months out, or I'll mark in my calendar to call you in a month or two.*

And this example is one you can use to just stay in touch—it doesn't require the other person to do anything, even respond.

> *It's been a long time since we've talked, but your name came up the other day when I was meeting with Vanessa Matthews. We, of course, said really nice things about you! I hope you're doing well and that business is good. Stay in touch!*

Building Ties with Allies

Your peers—the people who have roughly the same experience and connections as you—can be a great source of information about your field. And you never know when one of them will be promoted or hired into a position where they might have need of your skills. Here are some ways to deepen relationships with your allies:

- Ask a different colleague to breakfast, lunch, coffee, or drinks once a month or even once a week.
- Attend department after-work events (e.g., happy hour or golf games). Show up at least for a while, even if you're uncomfortable. Smile, ask open-ended questions, and listen—this is often where projects get hatched and decisions are made.
- Share the credit. Make sure there is plenty of "we" in your conversations and not too much "I."

Find Reasons and Ways to Connect

Develop a habit of reading periodicals and online news—read the "People Moving" sections of journals and news magazines, which helps you stay on top of what your network is doing and also makes you a better student of the game. Be observant of what's happening around you.

Send congratulatory notes to people who have new jobs, are in new organizations, or whose companies or employees have accomplished something great. E-mails are fine, but handwritten notes and cards are also very nice. One habit to adopt is to do one e-mail, note, or phone call every morning when you open your e-mail. LinkedIn makes this easy by sending you updates several times a week on people's birthdays, anniversaries, and job changes. It's easy to look at this each morning and send a quick e-mail acknowledging the occasions.

Acknowledge other people. Say, "Thank you." A lot. All the time. In person, on paper, digitally—mix it up. It's amazing how many people don't practice this simple courtesy. Don't join their ranks. Let all those you encounter know you appreciate their help. In our fast-paced world, taking a minute to say thank you goes a long way.

Nancy once was invited to a big lunch hosted by a search person. A few days slipped by before she realized she hadn't sent a thank-you note. She felt terrible about sending a late note but did it nonetheless . . . and she got a personal call back. The search person said she was the only one from his table of ten who had taken the time to send or call in a thank-you.

In our fast-paced world, taking a minute to say thank you goes a long way.

You will stand out if you say thanks!

Follow up and let people know what happened. If someone helps you out, follow up to let her know how it helped you or the impact it made. If someone referred you to someone else, send him an e-mail about the outcome (in positive terms). We have helped literally hundreds of people in their job searches; one thing that always surprises us is the number of people who don't even tell us they found a job—they just fade away.

While e-mail, letters, and phone calls are helpful for staying in touch, remember that networking is a contact sport. Use e-mail and social media judiciously—they can help you stay in touch with others, but they have limitations when it comes to strengthening relationships. Using social media is not the same as networking. Social media is only a tool to help you build and maintain your connections. LinkedIn is a great tool, but it doesn't work very hard for you if you don't follow up.

Be sure you build some face time into your week or month so you can deepen relationships through personal attention.

Be generous. Don't keep score on how much you give to a person and how much you receive in return. With some people, you will be the giver; with others, the receiver. If you approach your network with an attitude of abundance, it all evens out in the end.

HOW HENRY AND MEI EXPANDED THEIR NETWORKS

Henry, our IT job candidate, wants to be well prepared for his upcoming chance to talk with someone at Rent-A-Tech Corporation. He is looking at doing freelance work and learns that this might be one place where he could get some gigs. He does some research on Rent-A-Tech so he can have more interesting conversations. He reviews their website and also sees that three of his LinkedIn connections have contacts at Rent-A-Tech. He wants to find out more about the types of clients and projects at Rent-A-Tech. He also wants to know how busy they might keep him. He lists some questions, practices making conversation, and focuses on how he can best present himself.

He then contacts all three of his LinkedIn connections and asks if they would introduce him to the people from Rent-A-Tech. When he attends a professional meeting, he asks others if they know anything about Rent-A-Tech—and finds that they know a lot. When he asks if they would connect him with someone at Rent-A-Tech, they all say yes. He also asks what other firms work with contract software developers and hears about Catalysts in Technology; he even gets some referrals into that company.

Henry follows up on these new contacts at Catalysts and Rent-A-Tech. In his meetings, he says, "I've been getting to know a lot about your culture from other IT people, and they speak very highly of the company and the people who work there. I have great experience, but I want to work in more cutting-edge technology. What does it take to be able to work on those types of projects as a contractor?"

It's amazing what people will tell you when you're not asking for a job—you're just doing research! He also asks for leads on whom else he should talk with at Rent-A-Tech and Catalysts, along with some tips about how best to approach them. He gets a lot of helpful advice. Things are looking up.

You may remember that Mei landed a job in HR at Acme Corp. Prior to being hired, she, like Henry, wanted to be well prepared for the chance to talk with someone at the company. Many of Acme's employees had lunch at her restaurant, so she did some research on Acme so she could engage them in more interesting discussions. She practiced making conversation and thought about how her questions might affect her presentation.

The next time she had a table of customers from Acme, she said, "We get a lot of customers from Acme, and they are without exception really nice. It seems like a great company. People always speak very highly of it. Where do you all work?" One person from their party responded, "We work in the HR department. We're all in town for the annual meeting—and I'm so glad to hear our employees have good things to say!"

Mei responded, "Oh, they do. Your company seems to treat people well, which is not as common as it should be!"

Another guest then commented, "You seem to know a lot about it!"

Mei took charge. "Yes, my degree is in human resource management, and I've been getting to know a lot about your culture from my customers. It's amazing what people will tell you when you're just a friendly waitperson! Anyway, I would love to come over and meet with you at some point to learn more about the company and get some advice about how I might eventually transition out of this work and into the HR professional role I've trained for. Would any of you talk with me?" Needless to say, they said yes, and now Mei is an employee.

Look at how Henry and Mei presented themselves: confident, friendly, engaged, curious, passionate, qualified, ambitious. Who wouldn't want to talk with them?

CREATE AND NURTURE A NETWORK OF ADVOCATES

Mei, Natasha, George, and Henry have one thing in common, despite being at very different points in their careers: none of them has advocates.

Advocates are those people who think you are so terrific that they sing your praises to others, talk positively about you, or recommend you, often without even being asked. Marcia Ballinger and Nathan Perez call them your "evangelists," and Betsy Buckley, a nationally known coach, also calls them "ambassadors." Whatever the term, advocates are like gold—very precious—and therefore need to be nurtured.

Perhaps the best way to understand what we mean by advocates is through one of Nancy's experiences. Almost twenty years ago, Nancy was having a networking lunch with an acquaintance in the search firm business (whom she knew through committee work at her church). She wanted to learn more about that business and perhaps get some names of other headhunters. In the course of the conversation, her lunch partner said, "I have a friend whom I think you should meet. I don't know why, but I think you'd like each other. I think the world of him. His name is Mark LeBlanc." The following week, one of Nancy's clients who had his own businesses said, "My wife and I just started working with a business coach whom we really like. His name is Mark LeBlanc." Nancy hadn't asked for a referral; they just offered that information because they were advocates for Mark. That's what advocates do.

Hearing a name twice in one week left Nancy feeling she had to meet this guy! She got his phone number and left him a message, saying, "The universe has said we must meet. Your name has come up from several people, and I'd like to meet you." Note that this was a cold call warmed up by reference to the two people who had advocated for him. Mark called back, they had breakfast, and they soon became friends and professional colleagues, to their mutual benefit. They still refer business to each other. Thus, one advocate's reference gave Nancy and Mark each a new advocate, as well as more business.

Advocates send business to consultants, link people in transition to jobs, and help employees land promotions. Every new advocate can lead to a big payoff in your networking efforts.

How do you find an advocate? Your advocates are already in your network, currently as allies or even acquaintances—it's just a matter of strengthening those relationships. You don't ask someone to be your advocate—you build a relationship with a person over time until she or he becomes an advocate. Some people are natural and enthusiastic promoters of other people; they are more likely to become advocates than people who are not networkers or connectors themselves. You'll develop a good feel for who in your network would likely be an advocate for you.

MENTORS VS. ADVOCATES

When people think of advocates, they often think of mentors. They are not the same and shouldn't be confused. A mentor can be an advocate, but not all mentors will be advocates, and many advocates are not mentors. Mentors are typically experienced and trusted advisers, teachers, counselors, and guides, and they are typically very interested in helping people along in their career. However, they do not necessarily promote you or take action on your behalf.

Natasha, our marketing director, learned early on how *not* to develop an advocate. At a very early point in her career, she decided she needed an advocate, and who better than an executive of her own company? So she got an appointment on the EVP's calendar and straight-out asked if he would be her mentor and advocate. Now, he was not known as a great developer of people, and he was really busy, so he gave her a gentle turndown. (Better than a nasty rejection, but a downer nonetheless!) He was certainly the wrong person to ask, but this cold approach isn't likely to be successful in any scenario. First of all, being an advocate sounds like a lot of work to busy people who are not already invested in your career. You must build strong connections with people before expecting them to advocate for you, and it needs to emerge naturally because they think highly of you.

Early in his career, Richard took a different approach with the person he wanted as an advocate. They were at the same meeting, and the end of the meeting, he asked that person if he had time for a quick request for advice (obviously one Richard had prepared in advance). Then, after he'd acted on that advice, Richard *followed up* with that person to say thank you and tell him how it worked. That person was impressed Richard had taken the advice and had also made the time to get back to him. After that, you can be sure that person took Richard's e-mails and calls. Eventually he became an advocate and mentor, even without being formally asked or "titled" as such. (In fact, that same person has been helpful in getting this book off the ground.)

Advocates do not have to be senior executives or in positions of power, although it is nice if they are. They can be peers, bosses, customers, vendors, or people who report to you. They can come from any walk of life. Find advocates in your organization, profession, industry, and community, depending on your career direction and goals. Here are some ways in which you can develop advocates:

- Think about each of your advocates or potential advocates individually: what does each do for you, and what are her or his interests? This will give you some ideas about how to stay in touch with each advocate and continue deepening or strengthening the relationship.

- Plan to have *at least* three interactions with each advocate or potential advocate during the course of a year. Some relationships will allow—or require—more than that in a year.
- Think about what you can do for them—that is, actively advocate for your advocates and potential advocates. Look for chances when you can speak up for them, say something good about them, or pass their names on to search firms, customers, and so on.

Connecting with Advocates

Use a variety of media to stay in touch with your advocates—voicemail, e-mail, cards. For no reason other than you were thinking of them, write very thoughtful notes about how much you appreciate what they've done for you. Shoot off quick e-mails saying you were thinking of them when you read something about their organizations or interests of theirs. Be sure to thank them if an advocate does something for you—a call, a note, whatever is appropriate.

Other ideas for connecting include:

- Pay close attention to LinkedIn updates to watch for changes in their statuses or intriguing posts they initiated. Send notes or call to compliment or congratulate them. Mark LeBlanc is especially good at this—it's always nice to go into voicemail and hear his voice.
- Send an article or book you've found particularly good. (If you have the funds, you could send a copy to each of your advocates, making contact with them all in one easy step!) An occasional gift might be appropriate at times. A $10 gift card from a local coffeehouse or a ticket to an event is a nice touch for someone who's been especially helpful (depending on who they are).
- Ask for advice or help (as Richard did at the meeting).
- Attend an event an advocate will be at and make a point of connecting.

Take a minute and think through your network of acquaintances and allies. Are there any potential advocates in those lists? Jot down a few well-connected and natural networkers you'd like to get to know a lot better. What might be your next step in connecting with them?

NATASHA'S SUCCESS

Natasha really wants to stay in her company, and she also wants to continue advancing her career internationally. After learning that many of the senior leaders did not know her well, she knows she needs to gain a few advocates in senior positions. She still stings from her early-career attempt to get a mentor, but she has learned a lot since then.

Taking a smarter approach to creating new advocates, she sets up a meeting with her boss. She reminds him of her career hopes—that she wants to progress but also wants to stay with the company. She asks him what she needs to work on to earn a promotion, what he thinks her next steps should be, and which other senior leaders he recommends she get to know better. When he mentions two names, she next asks if he would grease the skids to help her connect with them.

Her boss agrees to set her up with the two senior contacts, and Natasha follows through with them, plus two others she approached on her own. In all, they include her boss's boss, the head of sales in another business unit, the SVP of talent development, and the EVP of sales in her own unit. She does her research and prepares good questions for each meeting, including how each person had navigated this company and others, and what advice each has for her in terms of next steps. She is pleased when the head of sales in another business unit says, "You know, I'm part of an informal group of senior women who meet for wine after work about once a month. Would you be interested in joining me next week?" Would she! Natasha is thrilled and thinks perhaps she has an advocate-in-the-making. She immediately sends a thank-you note and attaches an article they had discussed during the meeting.

Natasha is now much more confident in her career prospects, and of the eight people she meets over a few months, she feels she has good ideas for following up with five of them.

STAYING CONNECTED WITH YOUR NETWORK

We've given you some ideas about how to build relationships with new people, old acquaintances, and current and would-be advocates. If you've tried some of our ideas for building relationships, you should have the start of a very strong network of connections who can help you—and whom you can help. And hopefully you'll come to appreciate what strong relationships can do for your life, and you'll nurture them naturally as part of your daily routine.

You'll come to appreciate what strong relationships can do for your life, and you'll nurture them naturally as part of your daily routine.

However, as career counselors working with job seekers, we have both seen too many people work hard to build a network and then simply stop after they've found new jobs—only to have to resurrect their network once they're in need of help again. In this cycle, it becomes even more difficult to approach some people. So it pays off to stay in touch over time and not have to rebuild your network each time you need one.

Ways to Stay Connected

It's easiest to stay in touch with people when you're not asking for something. It's a matter of building a few new habits if you haven't already been doing this. So, what can you do to keep your network vital? Here are a few ideas that have worked for us and for others.

- Review, revamp, and refresh your network regularly. Once or twice a year, take stock of the quantity, diversity, and depth of your network. Put a plan in place to enrich your relationships, and make an effort to identify a new, small habit that will help you expand and strengthen the network.

- Be systematic in your approach. Do something weekly, monthly, or quarterly in order to keep your network alive in all areas—acquaintances, allies, and advocates.
- Have a system to organize your relationships and network contacts, including a weekly or monthly list of people with whom you need to touch base. This is where your contact database will be helpful.
- If you read a good article, send it to some of your allies or advocates interested in that topic.
- Send holiday (or birthday) cards. Sympathy cards are particularly appreciated when someone in your network has suffered a loss. Nancy keeps a supply of congratulations and sympathy cards—even cards on the loss of a pet—so she can send them easily and quickly and save herself an extra trip to the store.
- Give compliments and show appreciation to others. Regularly. Receive compliments gracefully.
- Make phone calls just to say hello and tell people you're thinking about them and why. Add compliments, if possible.

At the end of any networking conversation or meeting, ask if you can stay in touch. This leaves the ball in your court, and it means you don't have to be uncomfortable about contacting them in the future. Very few people will turn down this request. For example, you can say:

- "I'll keep you posted on my learnings. May I call you sometime if I have a question about ________?"
- "Do you mind if I check back with you periodically—every few months—just to see if you've learned anything new about_________?"
- "Thanks for taking the time to talk with me about ______, Mr. Smith. I've learned a lot and have found it very helpful in moving forward on the ____ project. I can see why Jane

Doe suggested I meet with you. Is there anything I can do for you? Would you mind if I keep in touch with you and contact you if I have questions in the future?"

Use E-Mails to Stay Connected

E-mail is one of the most common methods businesspeople use to stay connected. The following are some real-world samples.

One of Nancy's connections recently wrote:

Nancy—

Just a quick note of thanks for all your assistance. I've landed a contract position as interim CEO at__________. It's not likely a long-term role but is a great fit for now (and it feels great to be busy again!). Your referral to Mary Smith and follow-up connections led me to reposition my search and consider contract positions.

I hope this note finds you well. They say 70 degrees next week—tough to believe as I sit here watching it snow and see the forecast says there is more on the horizon!

Thanks again, Nancy, and btw, the team at __________ may touch base with you. I believe you know the founders, Pete and John—your name came up in conversation recently (in a good way).

Nancy recently sent this note to an ally in her network:

Dear Paul—

Thanks so much for your phone call yesterday. The information you shared was timely, and I was able to use it today in a meeting.

I hope things are going well for you this quarter—I know that things are tough in your industry right now.

By the way, I was having a cup of coffee with Mary Smith the other day, and your name came up—Mary spoke extremely highly of you—said you were a "real class act." And I couldn't agree more. Always nice to know when people are saying good things about you!

Stay in touch!

Develop and Practice Great Follow-up Habits

Meeting with people once does not build a relationship—you need to follow up and plan for additional contact. It is helpful to make a habit of meaningful follow-ups right after a meeting:

- Keep careful track of all your follow-up action items: What did you commit to doing, and what did others say they would do? When you have done your own follow-up actions, you may want to drop the other person an e-mail. (You can use your contact database for this!)
- Make a note of appropriate ways to stay on people's radar and at the top of their list, and schedule some follow-up actions.
- Circle back to the person who referred you to this most recent network contact; let her or him know what happened and how helpful it was.

NETWORKING CHALLENGES

Introverts

We would guess that, through most of this section on building relationships, introverts have been thinking, "That's all well and good for those extroverts, but I'm an introvert, and I can't do some of this stuff!" Here are some common concerns introverts face:

- They worry they're not good at small talk; they don't know how to warm up the conversation and get it flowing.
- Their minds go blank when they are trying to say the right thing. Their best lines come to them in the car after a meeting.

- Because they need to think things out before they speak, they wait too long to enter a conversation.

As introverts ourselves, we encounter every one of those challenges! But we also challenge introverts who use those concerns as an excuse to not build connections. Anyone—even the most staunch introvert— can adapt almost any of these strategies and tactics to fit his or her own style.

In fact, being an introvert has several advantages when building relationships. In her book *Quiet*, Susan Cain says that many qualities of introverts actually provide an advantage in building trustworthiness and credibility:

- As we've said, meaningful, trusting relationships are primarily built one-on-one. This is where introverts can shine!
- Introverts are usually better listeners than talkers—a distinct advantage in the types of conversations that lead to stronger relationships.
- Networking is about showing interest and asking questions of other people—introverts are usually better at this.
- While building a network is usually a face-to-face process, many of those relationships get started through e-mail or voicemail, giving introverts a foot in the door before they have to meet in person.
- Introverts may be better researchers—armed with knowledge, introverts can speak intelligently about trends and issues impacting their industry or profession.

Here are a few ideas that may be particularly helpful to introverts:

Practice breaking the ice with people you don't know well. In our chapter on working the room, you will find a number of questions and opening lines that are great conversation starters. Find three or four that fit your style for general purposes, and find something that fits a particular event you will be attending.

- *Practice introducing yourself.* "Hi, my name is . . ."
- *Hone your listening skills* if they need improvement. This will help you stay focused on the other person and ready to ask follow-up questions.
- *Find an event buddy.* If the thought of entering a room full of strangers is too much for you, find someone who will join you. This way you have backup—and it also means you can't back out at the last minute. Agree that you will not stay together at the event after you've both gotten your sea legs.
- *Get a work assignment.* If you will be attending an event, get an assignment, such as registering people or handing out programs or nametags. It gives you a natural platform to talk with people and eases the need for small talk that many of us dread.

If you're looking for a group to join but don't find one that fits, start a small group of people who meet for breakfast once a month to talk about a topic of interest. It could be as simple as a book group that reads books on leadership or a particular professional topic. You can start with just a couple of people and over time ask others to join.

Henry started a group of his own. As he was networking, he heard all kinds of opinions on Cloud technology and what comes after the Cloud. He asked several people involved in these conversations if they would be interested in having breakfast once a month to share information and developments in Cloud technology. They called it What's After Cloud Technology, or WACT. Along the way, they found another group of people discussing something similar about leading-edge technology, so they joined forces and are now a group of twenty-five. Henry has many more high-quality connections now, as well as a hotline to new information in his field.

Networking Under the Radar

Sometimes it's important to keep your networking confidential—for example, when an employed person is looking for a job at a different company. The process for networking under the radar is the same as that described above. However, you may need a cover story for your efforts. Here are some ideas that others have used successfully:

- Attend industry meetings and build relationships in the organizations that interest you. This can easily be positioned as professional development, which is good for your company: you gather new information and ideas, apply it to your work, and share what you're learning. Many organizations reward this type of engagement. Meanwhile, you can build numerous new relationships.
- Find or create a research project about a professional topic that allows you to interview people in targeted organizations. It needs to be a real project, of course—linked to your job, company, or professional association. Be sure to prepare strategic questions that show your knowledge. Reach out to industry leaders and conduct interviews to gather information. As you write the article, you can reconnect with contacts to secure authorization to use quotes, offer them the chance to provide feedback before publication, and so on. Then send out the final copy with a personal note of thanks. You can continue to build on those relationships with future publications or projects as well.
- Wear your business development "hat" to broaden your network. Many organizations encourage their employees to participate in business development. If you reach out to potential prospects under the guise of educating them about your organization, you can add value to your organization. Who knows? You might be instrumental in making a sale. That doesn't hurt your reputation, and you've also built a relationship that might be helpful, should you decide to move on.

We hope we've given you enough good reasons to build and maintain your network and some ideas for dipping your toe in the networking waters. We know it can be done, because we have done it throughout our careers. You can too!

TAKE ACTION TO POWER YOUR CAREER

Relationships are key. We all need others to help us get where we want to go. So if you really want to power your career with the best fuel, spend a bit more time each week paying attention to deepening your network.

- Find a way to build network maintenance into your daily, weekly, and monthly schedule—two to four hours per month will produce amazing results. Put it on your calendar.
- Keep your network fresh, vital, and helpful by continuing to add new acquaintances, allies, and advocates.
- Pick out two acquaintances and two allies to contact this week and meet with in the next month.
- Don't be afraid to develop advocates. They don't have to know you think of them that way—just treat them that way. Pick out one ally you'd like to have as an advocate and develop a strategy to move the relationship in that direction.

CHAPTER 8

MAXIMIZE EXECUTIVE CONTACTS

The boss. To fail to make that relationship one of mutual respect and understanding is to miss a major factor in being effective.

—John Kotter and John Gabarro

Imagine stepping into an elevator with the CEO of your company. You have only a few moments to engage her and let her know who you are. Are you ready to say something appropriate, or do you settle for standing there, staring at the door for twenty floors? How often have you wanted to say something to people but settled for complimenting them on their clothing or briefcase?

Nancy had this kind of opportunity early in her career: a thirty-seven-floor elevator ride with the CEO of her company. What an opportunity! However, she wasn't prepared, so they talked about the weather. At the end of that ride, he didn't know anything distinguishing about her (other than that she didn't like hot weather), and worse, he didn't even know her name.

In the previous chapters, we've addressed building a broad network of all types of individuals, depending on our goals. However, in almost any career, key types of strategic relationships are those cultivated with senior executives. These people can be incredibly helpful in our careers. Most of us would like to be known by people in senior roles in our organizations or professions. After all, isn't that how some people get promoted? Unfortunately, many of our jobs do not create many chances for talking to, presenting to, or interacting with the top brass. However, as Nancy's example above illustrates, small opportunities do pop up, and a tactful self-promoter anticipates these moments and is prepared to make an impact when they appear.

When do those opportunities appear? Some are serendipitous, and some are planned.

THE SERENDIPITOUS MEETING

Amazingly, many executives are not good at small talk themselves. Some are shy introverts. Some don't want to intimidate others. Some are simply arrogant. But virtually everyone will engage in a conversation if there is an appropriate opening—and we sometimes have to provide the opening.

Few of us are naturally skilled in being spontaneous in these types of situations. Being prepared for these moments can go a long way to making them more natural, comfortable, and effective. Here are several common situations and some ways to prepare for them.

An Executive Who Doesn't Know You

Imagine you run into a senior person in your company with whom you haven't had contact. Your goal is to connect your name with your value to the company in the executive's memory.

- Introduce yourself, using some version of your positioning statement:

"Hello, Ms. Executive. I'm Mei Johnson, I'm a ______________ in the human resources department working on _____ project. It's a pleasure to meet you, Ms. Executive."

or

"Hello, Mr. Executive. I'm John Smith—I'm the receptionist in the customer service area. I make sure everyone who contacts the company has a great first impression. It's a pleasure to meet you."

- Introduce yourself, tying your name to a key project in the organization or to the name of your leader or team:

"Hello, ________________. I'm George Harrison. I work with John Jones in the finance department, and I'm on the ERP project. We've made some good progress this month."

or

"Hello, ______________. I'm Mei Johnson. I work on Project Nebraska, and we really appreciate the endorsement the senior team gave us last week. Thank you."

- Introduce yourself, complimenting the executive or the company on some public achievement, or on your good experience there:

"Hello, Mr. Bigwig. I'm ______________. I work in the ________ department, and I just want you to know that I love working at this company! I'm proud of our products and love working for Mikah Jones in marketing."

What executive isn't going to ask you more questions in the time available? Be prepared with a few details about why you like the company.

- Introduce yourself, and compliment one of the executive's employees who has been helpful to you:

"Hello, Ms. Bigwig. I'm ___________. I work in _____________, and I just want you to know that Maria Espinosa in your department has been a savior for us this month. She expedited an order, and it made a real difference for us with a difficult customer."

An Executive Who Knows You

Now imagine running into a senior person in your company or another company who *does* know you. Say something of interest to them.

- Tie what you are doing to one of the senior person's projects:

  "Hello, Kim! I haven't seen you at the meetings recently, but I wanted to say how much I appreciate being on the ERP team. I'm learning an unbelievable amount about the workings of other departments."

- Give a compliment about results or strategy:

  "Hi, Juan. I listened to the town meeting last week and heard about the great third-quarter results. Congratulations! I appreciate keeping up to date with the business through those town meetings."

- Comment on an issue important to the senior person:

  "I've read about the work you do on the board of the Red Cross, and I admire it greatly . . . I think highly of the Red Cross, and I have been thinking of volunteering there."

- Thank the person for something done or said on behalf of the company:

  "Thank for the compliments you gave to all employees for their effort on helping achieve great third-quarter results. My staff really appreciated it."

Being prepared for these serendipitous occurrences requires you to be a student of the game. That is, you must be interested enough in your company or your industry to have a general sense of what's going on and what some of the priorities and results are. Of course, you can't be prepared with information specific to everyone you run into. But if you know a few key pieces of information, you can be prepared for a brief conversation that establishes at least a nodding relationship with any senior executive.

Being prepared for these serendipitous occurrences requires you to be a student of the game.

WHAT DO EXECUTIVES ACTUALLY THINK ABOUT EMPLOYEES WHO PROMOTE THEMSELVES?

A senior executive of a healthcare company recently commented on getting to know employees at lower levels in the organization. He said he had gotten to know several employees because they had struck up conversations with him.

One in particular is Juan, a member of the maintenance staff. He often runs into Juan when walking from the parking lot to the office. One morning, Juan told the executive he had bought a few shares of stock in the company and that he keeps up on it. Occasionally, Juan will mention something he's read or heard about recent company performance. This executive appreciated his commitment and willingness to engage.

The executive also mentioned that he notices employees who participate in company events outside of work. For example, once his company sponsored an event promoting good health and raising money for a nonprofit. He noticed one employee in particular, Margie—whom he knew only slightly. They didn't talk at the event, but he now pays more attention to what she does.

He commented that, if either of these two employees ever approached him for a favor, he would be very willing to help them out, if he could.

Additional Tips

- If you work in a field office and will be making a trip to your headquarters, set up a meeting with one new senior person you'd like to get to know and learn from. (And of course, prepare some good questions!)
- Know the interests of some key executives in your organization, particularly those in your own functional area or business unit.

- Be sure you know the executives in your organization by both face and name. You can't connect with them if you don't even know who they are! At the least, become familiar with your boss's boss and his or her peers in your functional area.
- Do your research: read company literature (even those annual reports!) and attend events to stay up to date on company, industry, and competitors' issues.

Henry, the IT job hunter, has done his homework: he talked with people at Rent-A-Tech, looked at their website, checked them out on LinkedIn and Glassdoor, and googled for articles about them. He now knows he is very interested in connecting with Rent-A-Tech and can ask a few pertinent questions. He also read their annual report and knows a few executive faces.

One day Henry is in line at a coffee shop in the high-tech district of the city when he recognizes a Rent-A-Tech top executive. He gathers up his courage and says, "Aren't you Krishna Patel, one of the executives at Rent-A-Tech? I've been doing a lot of research on your company, and everyone I talked with said they all love working with and for your company. You must be doing many things right to have so many speak so positively about you!"

Notice that Henry knew Mr. Patel's name and his role. He paid him a compliment and didn't ask him for anything. He could have opened by stating that he was looking for work, but he decided it could wait. Luckily, his approach impresses Mr. Patel enough that he asks Henry why he was doing so much research. Henry then tells him he is looking for work. Henry is thrilled when Mr. Patel offers his card and says, "Give me a call tomorrow." You can be sure this is one phone call Henry will make promptly!

George, the financial consultant, has a somewhat similar experience. During an after-work gathering at a downtown bar, one of George's acquaintances introduces him to another acquaintance of hers. Because he has been doing so much research on potential companies, George immediately recognizes the new person as the CFO of Meridian Corporation. He doesn't share his value proposition yet but instead says he knows Meridian is going through an ERP conversion. When the CFO asks how he knows, he replies that he has recently started his own consulting business and that one of his strengths is leading complex, troubled projects on time and on budget. (He had heard Meridian's conversion was a little bumpy.) Her eyes get big, and she says, "We need to talk!" They exchange contact information, and he is in her office before the end of the week.

THE PLANNED MEETING WITH AN EXECUTIVE

Hoping exclusively on serendipity may mean waiting a long time to add senior leaders to your network. Although some people seem to run into senior executives all the time, the rest of us can create opportunities to make this happen. You may have to work to find ways to get exposure to your boss's peers, your boss's boss, and that person's peers (as well as higher-level executives).

Natasha is one of the best examples of someone making things happen in this arena. After learning many of the senior leaders had not endorsed her in the succession planning meeting, Natasha decided she had to do something to gain visibility. She talked it over with her manager, and he gave her some ideas and supported her in gaining an opportunity to write an article for the company's online news magazine. Researching it would require her to interview a number of the senior executives for their views on the international marketing challenges in the industry.

She made appointments for an hour with each of them over a one-month period. She researched like mad in order to ask strategic questions that would lead to dialogue and forge some stronger relationships. And of course, afterward she followed up with thank-you letters, noting some of the things she had learned in the course of her project. Over the course of the next several months, she also sent them a few additional articles.

Natasha's article was well received within the company, and she was asked to participate on a panel for an in-house company telecast. She got some extra coaching on her presentation skills and did a bang-up job, leading to more visibility for herself and her department. Finally, she decided to be bold and repeat this outside her company. She garnered a spot at an industry conference (they are always looking for relevant presenters), interviewed CEOs of several other companies, and compared that information with what she had heard from her own leaders. Her presentation went well, and she also used the opportunity to go back to her own company's executives and report what she had learned outside.

This was a real boon to Natasha's career as a leader in her company and her industry, and in addition helped her develop and enhance her presentation skills. The next time her name came up in a succession planning meeting, many of the executives in the room knew and thought of her well.

Sound farfetched? It's not. Successful people do it every day. Almost everyone has an opportunity to do some version of this. Even if you're an entry-level employee like Mei, there are similar ways to interact with your boss's peers or your boss's boss. Chapter 12 has more ideas you can modify for your own situation, but you can use these suggestions to get started connecting with higher-level people:

- Locate groups and communication vehicles in the organization and ask for your supervisor's help in how to best get involved in them.
- Ask to join a cross-functional team working on a business project—virtually all companies have these.
- Join a professional association or industry group consisting of people at your level and higher, so you can become comfortable interacting with people in senior roles.

Mei used this last idea for one of her efforts. After having been in her job for some time, Mei researched local human resources professional associations and found one with a number of senior HR people. She also found no end of volunteer jobs she could do: committee work, conference logistics, registration, and so on. She picked out a few and began meeting more high-ranking people.

Of course, if you use this tactic, remember that being worthy is absolutely key— you must be doing bang-up work in your primary job before you venture into this type of career effort.

ATTEND TO YOUR RELATIONSHIP WITH YOUR BOSS

Probably the most strategic relationship you can develop is with your own boss. While it's nice to think about enhancing relationships with top executives, your immediate boss can be a critical help to your career. Not everyone is gifted with a great boss or one with a lot of power in the organization, but even a poor boss may be helpful to your career. At the very least, you don't want your boss to damage your reputation.

Natasha was smart in leveraging her relationship with her boss. When she got an idea for a project, she talked it over with her boss and got support and ideas. In addition to the advice already discussed about working with your boss, keep in mind these ideas:

Meet Regularly with Your Boss or Manager

It may be standard procedure to meet regularly with your boss, or you may need to request meetings yourself. In either case, be prepared with an agenda and updates of your progress, and make sure your boss knows what value you bring to your department and the company. Know your boss's expectations and be respectful of his or her time.

Some bosses don't schedule regular one-on-one meetings with their staff members or are prone to frequently cancelling them. There is nothing wrong if you, the employee, request meetings or reschedule those cancelled—after all, it is in your best interests to have a strong relationship with your boss.

Get to Know Your Boss's Priorities

What is important to him or her? How can you help? For example, is your boss involved in a meeting or conference or on a nonprofit board? Is he or she leading a big project? Be aware of these things and offer to help (without taking on too much).

Ensure Your Boss Knows Your Career Objectives

Verbalize your career goals—short and long term. You can do this by telling your boss the next positions you're interested in and the longer-term career path you'd like, and then ask for advice on how to prepare and what timeframe to expect.

This was a painful lesson Jennifer, one of our former clients, learned. She was hoping (and waiting) for a promotion that just didn't come. Finally, she gathered up the courage to talk with her manager and told him she was really interested in a specific job. He was shocked—for some reason, he hadn't realized Jennifer was interested in a promotion, particularly into another department. But he did think highly of her and her work, so over the next six months, he helped make it happen. Don't assume your boss knows your career goals—communicate them directly!

Ask for Your Manager's Feedback, Advice, and Support

Jennifer's story illustrates how very positive results can come when you clearly communicate with your boss. However, sometimes asking for support leads to some tough feedback. Maybe you think you're ready for a promotion, but your boss is looking for improvement first in your current performance. But even that can be a gift disguised in a painful package. What better time than right now to find out how you need to improve? Better now than many years later, when your career has not unfolded as you had hoped.

Or perhaps you and your boss will find you have different opinions about your next career move. Even if you decide not to take your boss's advice, it is still worthwhile to discuss your ideas with him or her. It's a way to get another data point, another perspective. And most importantly, it'll show your boss that you respect him or her enough to seek out advice and make your goals clear.

Pass along Good Feedback

When you get a compliment (often by e-mail) from a coworker or customer, forward it to your boss. Someone else's words can be much more powerful than just giving a report. Don't overdo this one, however—too many of these in the boss's inbox can become an irritant. And make sure the accomplishment is worth passing on.

Make Sure Your Boss Sees Your Enthusiasm and Energy

Most of us want to see energy in our coworkers, and bosses are certainly no different. Frame your comments in ways that show enthusiasm for the department goals (even if you may not feel it inside!). Practice talking about your job in positive ways rather than negative complaints. Build on your boss's ideas rather than being oppositional.

Nancy really blew one situation early in her career. Her boss had been leading the planning for the "conference of his dreams," as he called it, with speakers he really wanted to hear talking together. At the last minute, business kept him back, and he offered Nancy an opportunity to attend in his place. It was really good! However, instead of preparing a nice report that summarized all the high points, Nancy just said, "Fine," when he asked her how it went. The look on his face said it all—he had been expecting to hear about all the things that went on at the conference, and "fine" just didn't cut it. It didn't enhance their relationship!

Be Seen as a Trustworthy Employee

Don't let your boss hear from someone else about what you're doing. Keep him or her informed on high-priority matters. If you're applying for a position within the company, let him or her know ahead of time. (This is required in some companies.) If you're volunteering for a task force or doing something to get visibility in the company or industry, give your boss the courtesy of a heads-up. And if something is going south, fair warning certainly is in order.

Say Thank You

Be sure to thank your boss when he or she does something to help you out. This seems like a no-brainer, but many managers tell us they don't often hear back from people for whom they've gone to bat. After managers pass out bonus checks or raises, only a small minority expresses gratitude. So even if you feel you've earned it or had hoped for more support, find a way to express your gratitude nevertheless.

One lovely example of someone who did this was a semiretired executive who worked part time for our firm. When it came to bonus time, he received a (very) modest check. He still took the time to write a note to the general manager. He said that even though he had often received much, much larger bonuses, and even though this was the smallest bonus he had ever received, he appreciated it more than any other because he knew how difficult a year it had been and how hard the GM had fought to get the money. You can be sure that GM remembers that note and that person positively!

Many managers tell us they don't often hear back from people for whom they've gone to bat.

THE INEFFECTIVE BOSS

If your boss is not well thought of in the company, it's still worth building a good relationship. However, you also might want to respectfully build relationships with a few peers of your boss, your boss's boss him or herself, or the peers of your boss's boss. It never hurts to have more than one advocate!

So, starting with your immediate boss and going up the ladder, it's worth building relationships with people senior to you in the organization. We hope you've found some ways of connecting that you can make work for you. If you start with our ideas and find a few that fit your style and time availability, you'll go a long way toward promoting yourself!

TAKE ACTION TO POWER YOUR CAREER

A career is ultimately powered by relationships, and it helps if some of those relationships are in more senior roles. It's never too early, or too late, to start cultivating authentic relationships with people of influence.

- Be prepared for serendipitous opportunities to build relationships with people higher up in your organization, industry, and profession.
- Create an opportunity to connect with people in senior roles in your organization, industry, and profession this month.
- Build a strong, communicative relationship with your boss.

SECTION THREE

INCREASE YOUR VISIBILITY

INCREASE YOUR VISIBILITY

Opportunity is missed by most people because it is dressed in overalls and looks like work.

—Thomas A. Edison

Once you are comfortable talking about your value and you've ignited your network, you can look at additional ways to elevate your visibility. You have to increase your visibility, which means you need to become known beyond people you already know. This is when some of our clients resist. So before you slam the book shut (literally or figuratively), be assured that the techniques we'll teach are not beyond anyone's capabilities. In fact, much of this work is easier and less stressful than building a network, even for introverts. You don't need to speak in public, get on the radio, or launch a blog if you don't want to!

Before we lay out our strategies, let's check in with our four friends to see how their careers are progressing. As it turns out, they have all made progress with a few key connections, but they need to put some effort into increasing their visibility.

NATASHA, still a director of marketing, is more determined than ever to move up the ladder. She's built some good relationships with people higher up in her company, and she feels she's poised for the promotion she wants. In one of these conversations, she learned her lack of experience in Asia may reduce her chances of getting the job. She has plenty of experience in Latin America, much of which she believes is transferrable, but those in charge don't seem to think she has enough global experience. She wants to make her case, but she isn't sure what strategy would influence the decision makers.

GEORGE, our finance consultant, is making progress in his networking. He finally reached out and asked for help, and as a result he has secured a couple of good assignments. But he's still shocked when he runs into friends who have no idea he's started his own business. And he's discovered he has quite a bit of competition—people with more experience and more resources. He doesn't want to just underprice them because he is easily as skilled as they—and he needs the funds. He must differentiate himself, stand out as a real expert. But he's not quite sure how to go about it.

MEI, along with building some great relationships inside her company, has joined a professional association. But she's still not comfortable at the association meetings. She doesn't know what to say or how to meet new people. She attends nearly every month but leaves as soon as the presenter is done. She's learning something from the sessions but doesn't feel she's leveraging her membership. She doesn't know why the large group makes her nervous, as she does great in one-on-one meetings (once she finally gives them a try). She just doesn't like to work the room, but she knows she needs to get better at it if she wants relationships in her professional community. She's thinking about the next steps.

HENRY is interviewing for an exciting opportunity. One of his advocates referred him for a position and even spoke with the hiring manager on his behalf. He feels good about that, but his competition is an insider. He really wants this job and is looking for ways to stand out without being a pest. He knows he needs to keep networking until he has an actual offer.

It appears our friends could benefit by increasing their visibility. Like most of us, they need to become known beyond their personal network. There are some terrific ways to broadcast a personal brand, and in this section, we'll explore some great ways to increase your visibility and solidify your reputation beyond your personal contacts.

Here's what we'll cover in the next four chapters:

INCREASE YOUR VISIBILITY

- Make Meetings Matter and Learn to "Work a Room"
- Promote Your Team and Your Department
- Leverage LinkedIn and Social Media
- Be Seen as a Thought Leader

Chapter 9: Make Meetings Matter and Learn to "Work a Room"

Most people don't see daily and weekly meetings and conference calls as opportunities to build a reputation. But they are. So are professional conferences and networking events that give you the opportunity to meet new people and build your network. Don't worry—we'll help you feel confident when given the chance to "work the room" at an event! (Okay, so that may be a bit of an exaggeration, but we do have strategies that will make it easier.)

Chapter 10: Promote Your Team and Your Department

Your reputation is in part influenced by the reputation of the organizations with which you are affiliated. If your team is seen as exemplary, your personal reputation will be enhanced. There are many ways to elevate the visibility of a high-performing team or department by applying the art of tactful self-promotion. This is an essential skill if you are the leader of a team, department, or other enterprise, but even team members can put it to use.

Chapter 11: Leverage LinkedIn and Social Media

Obviously, it is important to build your brand online and gain exposure to a much larger professional community. What shows up if someone googles your name? What do people learn about you when they find you on LinkedIn? (And you'd better make sure the right people *are* finding you on LinkedIn!) We'll share some strategies for building your brand online and creating an online presence.

Chapter 12: Be Seen as a Thought Leader

Being seen as a thought leader can advance your reputation and career with surprising speed. You can do this by writing articles, a blog, special reports, or even a book. You can also consider public speaking or appearances as a guest on radio, television, or a relevant podcast. We'll share some key strategies for getting started in this arena, none of which are beyond your reach.

These chapters will provide you with practical ideas to help you become more visible and better heard within your organization, profession, and industry, so you can get the opportunities and recognition you deserve.

CHAPTER 9

MAKE MEETINGS MATTER AND LEARN TO "WORK A ROOM"

What people say and feel about you when you've left a room is precisely your job while you are in it.

—Rasheed Ogunlaru

In the past, George and Henry, being good introverts, took pride in avoiding as many meetings as possible. They felt so many meetings were unproductive and poorly organized, with the "blowhards" taking up too much time on the agenda. While this might be true too often, meetings *can* be very productive ways to get business done—as well as advance your visibility and your career. Part of this depends on how you approach them.

The truth is, meetings are a fact of life in today's organizations. Much of the time, you don't have a choice about which meetings to attend. So if you have to be there, why not use the time to elevate your reputation and enhance your image while completing the task at hand? And then there are other meetings you may actually *choose* to attend because you have an interest in the content or because you want to meet other people attending.

In this chapter, we'll talk briefly about routine meetings—those that happen every day or week, usually in-house. But we'll talk at greater length about large meetings and conferences. While building a network is primarily done one-on-one, group events may provide the first threads of a larger network of allies and acquaintances. We'll give you some guidance how to work the room at these networking meetings and cocktail hours.

ROUTINE MEETINGS

How you approach meetings is part of your brand and central to your reputation. Whether you *have* to attend or *choose* to attend, take a few minutes to prepare. Who else will be there? What positive contribution might you make? Imagine if everyone approached meetings this way. They would probably be much more productive! So there are lots of good reasons to model these behaviors.

How you approach meetings is part of your brand and central to your reputation.

The key behavior isn't complicated: just show up and pay attention instead of doing other work, playing games on your phone, or sitting by the door waiting to escape. Arrive on time or a little early. (Your punctuality is part of your brand.) Even if meetings in your organization never start on time, be there on time yourself. If you're concerned about wasting time during the delay, bring some reading material, but then promptly put it away when the meeting begins. That said, it's better to use that time before the meeting to engage with others—this is a prime networking opportunity.

When the meeting starts, say something useful within the first two minutes to make your presence known. Ask a question, offer an opinion, or give a compliment. This is a simple way to make sure you're visible. Of course, nobody likes the person who asks questions that have already been answered, restates the obvious, or holds up progress in order to debate some meaningless point. Go to the meeting with the intent of making it productive. If you have something to report or present, ask to be on the agenda. That puts your name in front of everyone's eyes (and makes it impossible for you to back out). If you work to add value to meetings, then they will become useful tools.

THE CHALLENGES OF WORKING REMOTELY

In this era of telecommuting, there's an increasing number of people working remotely. If you work remotely, you're faced with extra challenges in being able to promote yourself. You have fewer opportunities to "run into" someone and have a casual conversation. And rather than your physical presence, you depend on your voice to represent you. Here are a few suggestions for tactful self-promotion when working remotely:

- To make sure you're on people's radar, use instant messaging, e-mail, and the phone more often than you might otherwise.
- Don't just make calls when you have business to conduct. Make some calls just to connect socially. Of course, you'll want to keep these calls short, but consider them the equivalent of a chat at the water cooler. It's not a bad idea to create and regularly review a list of folks with whom you should connect.
- When you do go into the office, be intentional about seeing and connecting with a number of people (beyond just the meeting you're attending). Make a list before each visit to plan whom you should see.
- Be aware of how your voice comes across on the phone. Ask questions and make sure you are well prepared for every call. This is how people will know you.
- Be present during remote meetings. There is an extra temptation to multitask when you're on the phone and no one can see you, but it can easily detract from your participation.

If you are running a meeting or are asked to step in, take that role seriously. Plan ahead and create an agenda (get feedback, if appropriate and if time allows). Start the meeting on time. Make sure everyone knows each other—if not, prepare an introductory activity. How you handle group interaction will go a long way toward building your reputation with a lot of people. Specifically, you should develop some basic facilitation skills so you can effectively engage participants as well as handle resistance, objections, or questions. If you can run a meeting in a way that keeps people on task and engaged and doesn't waste everyone's time . . . can you imagine what good that can do for your reputation?

PROFESSIONAL MEETINGS AND CONFERENCES

Conferences or monthly meetings, whether in your industry or through professional associations, can be extremely helpful in your career. In many cases, however, they are not well used. At conferences in the past, George, Henry, and Mei (like many others) generally showed up at the large assembly, attended a few presentations, and then went home or to their hotel rooms. No wonder they didn't want to go to these events! But you can get a bigger payoff from these types of events if you do some strategic planning.

Before the Event

Whether you have a few days' or a few months' notice, you have plenty of time to plan for an event. Be sure to follow the event's website and updates so you can make the most of your time.

Decide which events you'll attend and which groups you'll join. For example:

- If, like Natasha, you are trying to connect with people in senior roles, select meetings that will be more strategic in nature, with executive presenters.

- If, like Henry, you are between jobs, attend only one meeting primarily attended by unemployed people, and then select other meetings attended by people currently working.
- If, like George, you are trying to start a business, consider one or more meetings attended by potential clients. For example, instead of just attending finance profession meetings, George might consider industry associations, the Chamber of Commerce, or Rotary meetings.

Doing a little planning in this regard will ensure your time is well spent!

Develop a strategy for each event. Think about the different gatherings you'll attend (seminars, roundtables, networking receptions, etc.) and decide on an approach for each. Ask yourself:

- What is my goal for this meeting?
- How many new people will I meet?
- Whom do I want to meet? Are there people attending that I should seek out?
- With whom will I reconnect?
- How can I help other people? (Because we know you can!)

Secure a specific role. Registering people, handing out nametags, being a greeter, even working the beverage table enables you to meet just about everyone, and it gives you built-in conversation starters. This is particularly helpful for introverts who haven't mastered the fine art of small talk. Having a role such as greeter often means your encounters must be brief, though. If you make special connections, tell those people you hope to meet up with them later at the event. But get their cards in case you don't get a chance!

Figure out whom you want to meet. Obtain a list of participants, speakers, vendors, or panelists and highlight those you want to hear and the topics you want to learn more about. Reach out to presenters by e-mail *before* the meeting in order to make initial introductions, so they will have a context of who you are when you approach them at the event. It is much easier to approach speakers if they know who you are or have at least heard your name. Do research on the presenter to personalize your correspondence.

Here's an example of an e-mail you might send to a speaker:

> *Hi, Ms. Jones. I'm Richard Dodson, a ______________ at ____________, and I will be attending the ____________ conference. I was really excited to read that you will be speaking. I'm interested in your topic because __________. I plan on attending your session, and I'd like to stop by and say hello.*

We both have had many occasions to speak at meetings and conferences. Invariably, many people come up to us before and after our presentations, wanting to connect. We have to say we pay more attention to people who have gotten in touch ahead of time to tell us who they are and why they are interested in our topic. We're much more likely to move a relationship forward with those people than with someone who just rushes up, shakes our hands, and wants to talk (and, heaven forbid, also doesn't have a business card).

Set up meetings ahead of time. Invite people for coffee or drinks at the event. Even better, bring several people together to connect over drinks or a meal. Here's an e-mail example of that contact:

> *Hello, Mary—*
>
> *I see from the list of participants that you'll be attending the____ conference. I'd love the chance to connect with you and learn more about how you landed at XYZ company. I wonder if you have time in your schedule to have breakfast (or lunch or a drink) so we could talk for 20–30 minutes. How about breakfast on Tuesday, the 21st? Thanks in advance. I look forward to seeing you.*

Practice your positioning statement. How will you introduce yourself to others at a cocktail party? How will you catch their ear and a share of their attention? Here are a few examples, along with their actual job titles:

"Hi, I'm __________. I help people get the best real estate on Google." (Search engine optimization expert)

"Hi, I'm _____________. I create a-ha moments for people who want to understand marketing data." (Market research specialist)

"Hi, I'm ________. I create learning that works, learning that fits, learning that lasts." (Learning and development consultant)

Get on the committee planning the event. Most recurring events are glad to have more volunteer help! You may even get a mention in the program or newsletter—good for name recognition. You'll also get to know some insiders in your company, industry, or profession and show them the value you bring.

During the Conference or Event

The actual event will be much easier and more productive if you've done some of the preparation.

- Go prepared with your business cards and introduce yourself. If you don't have business cards, have some made—you'll be surprised at how often you'll use them! Of course, you'll also want to be prepared to exchange your contact information electronically as well. In particular, seek out the people you contacted prior to the event and make introductions.
- When you talk with new people, ask for their contact information. Make notes for now—the date and where you met, the connection between you, what their interests are—and plan to enter everything into your contact database later. This information helps when you follow up (because, of course, you'll always follow up!).
- Be observant and judicious about how much time people may have to talk with you. Speakers are especially busy, and other attendees may have scheduled meetings, just as

you have. Don't overstay your welcome. Unless you've set up time for coffee or a meal, you should, as a general rule, spend no more than ten minutes with each person. When wrapping up, ask people if you can stay in touch.

- Whenever talking to people, focus on *them* . . . not *you*. Why are they attending, what do they want to get out of the event, what are their key challenges? Be present to them and maintain eye contact. Avoid looking around to see who else is at the event. Be attentive to how you can help other people. If you feel you can help them, the goal of such a conversation is to schedule a follow-up meeting.

After the Event

So, you spoke to a few great contacts and exchanged contact information. Now what? How you follow up after the event is probably the most important aspect of connecting—it's how you deepen the relationships you've started. Follow up that night or the next day. Here are a few ideas.

- Invite people to join you as LinkedIn contacts.
- Send e-mails saying how much you enjoyed meeting them. Mention something positive about them or the conversations. Suggest next steps that will continue to build the relationship.
- On social media, give a shout-out to the particularly interesting people you met.
- Arrange follow-up coffee meetings (your treat!) with those you'd like to get to know better. Send invitations where appropriate and always ask yourself, "How can I help them?"
- And of course, add their information to your contact database, with a reminder to reach out in the near future.

We want to emphasize that while group events can be helpful in meeting new people and starting important threads, they are not the best way to build strong relationships. You don't win awards for going to the most networking events. However, events can be great ways to 1) find new people with whom you'd like to build relationships, 2) stay connected to colleagues, and 3) keep learning about industry and professional issues. These events are very useful when you work them well and follow up!

LEARN TO WORK A ROOM

So there you are, at the event's networking reception. Most of us step into the room and immediately look for people we know and are comfortable with, and then we hang out with only them. And if we don't know anyone, then we're like singles at a party. We try to keep moving and try to look engaged, hoping someone will make eye contact or walk up to us and start talking. Either way, this type of "networking" meeting probably ends up being a waste of time.

Don't *assume* anyone will approach you to converse. Although it would be nice to think someone will approach you, it is unlikely. People tend to stick with their own friends in a crowd, even at networking events. Rather than waiting on others to approach you, become comfortable approaching others and starting conversations yourself. Remember, many people feel the same way you do—they wish they had someone to converse with, and you might be the answer to their prayers!

Find one other person who is alone and approach him or her. This lone wolf will be so grateful—he or she will think you're a wonderful person. When Nancy joined a new church many years ago, she did not know anyone. She still remembers with fondness the person who came up to her and introduced herself. Nancy still sees her and still tells her how much she appreciated what she did.

Ask open-ended questions, those that begin primarily with *what* or *how*. And get the other person to talk—people love to talk about themselves, and they'll think you're a wonderful conversationalist! Here are a few examples to get you started:

- "How long have you been a member of this group? Why did you join?"
- "Are you active? What do you feel you get out of being a member?"
- "What other groups do you belong to? What other groups would you recommend?"
- "Tell me about your organization. How is your business going?"
- "What challenges face your industry right now?"
- "How do you know________?" (if a mutual acquaintance is hosting the event)
- "How did you happen to get into __________?"
- "What do you like most about what you do?"
- "What other people do you know here?"
- "How can I help you? Is there anyone in particular I could maybe introduce you to?"
- "What do you enjoy doing outside of work?"

Break into a group that's already formed. The advantage of breaking into a group that's already going strong is that you don't have to say a lot (at least not until you're ready). You can listen and then chime in when you have something to add to the conversation, at which point you can introduce yourself. The tough part is edging into a group that is already talking. Here are a few things to try:

- Find an open spot and quietly say, "Mind if I join you?" Just listen—don't try to add your two cents or bring up your own topic until you understand what's going on within this conversation. Then ask a question.
- If you're given a chance, just say, "Hi, I'm _________, and I find this topic really interesting . . ."
- You even might try, "Hi. I don't know anyone else at this meeting. Mind if I join you?"

Act like a host. Assume some responsibility for others, as you would if you were hosting an event in your home. Find ways to help others succeed. Introduce people to others, mentioning a common interest between them.

WHAT JIM ASKED NANCY ON THEIR FIRST DATE

"What do you enjoy doing outside of work?" brings to mind a story: Nancy's husband, Jim, asked her that same question on their first date many years ago and still uses it with other people today. He always asks people, "What are your hobbies?" (Alternatives include "Do you have any hobbies outside of work?" or "What are your interests outside of work?") This absolutely opens people up—you learn a side of them you never would have guessed. It's also a good question when you are with a boss or executive and their partner—it truly draws people out and paves the way for many follow-up questions. Or if you're the boss, it can make you seem less intimidating to your employees and their partners. After many years of marriage and many group events, Nancy may be a little weary of hearing her husband's question, but it charms people and gets them to open up every time. Different questions will fit different situations—you get the idea!

Keep moving. Once you've made a connection, move on. This is sometimes an awkward part of mingling—feeling that you're stuck with someone for too long. Some ways to move on gracefully include:

- "I think we ought to connect later to talk in more depth. Here's my card."
- "Right now, I think we each need to work the room a bit and make another contact. Is there anyone in particular you want to meet?"
- "Tonight I've made it a goal to meet five new people. Is there anyone you think I ought to connect with?"
- "Have you tasted those hors d'oeuvres? I'm going to refresh my plate (or drink)."

- "Wow, do I ever need to find a restroom. Can you point me in the right direction?"

Exchange contact information. Pledge to make at least two new contacts during the networking session. Get their business cards or exchange ecards. Jot notes on them as to when and where you met, plus something that will remind you of your conversation. Transfer that information into your contact database as soon as possible after the event.

Group Event Don'ts

- Don't play the mind game and succumb to feeling like a fraud: "Everyone here knows each other. I don't feel I belong here." Replace these negative assumptions with positive self-talk: "I belong here, and everyone else does *not* know each other—meeting new people is *why we're here*!" There truly are many people who would like to get to know you.
- At a sit-down event, don't be the first to sit at a table. You will have no control over who sits down with you. Instead, move into the room slowly, walk around, and find a table where people are already sitting—preferably people you'd like to meet. Sit next to someone in whom you're particularly interested.
- Don't stay with people you already know, unless meeting new contacts as a group is your purpose for being there.
- Don't sit in the same place at every meeting. Vary your location in the room.
- Don't make a bad impression with your food and drink choices. Sloppy foods that drip and spill make you look unprofessional, and if your hands are full of plates and glasses, it's hard to pull out your card. And of course, avoid overindulgence in alcohol.

OUR FRIENDS SEE THE LIGHT!

To their credit, George, Henry, and Mei have opened themselves to different ways of doing things, and it's paying off!

Henry invests in some business cards with his contact information, his branding statement, and his differentiators, and he spends a few dollars on some attractive professional graphics. He contacts a number of IT people in his community and asks which organizations they find the most valuable professionally, then he researches those organizations online. He chooses one to start with and prepares some questions. He walks into the first meeting with trepidation but also with the belief that he can do this. And he does! During the thirty-minute networking period, he approaches six people, telling them he's new and asking them how long they've belonged to the organization, why they joined, what they got out of it, and what they recommend he do to get the most from his membership. He comes away with *five* new connections and an invitation to join the program committee. He's looking forward to meeting more people at the committee meeting and is ready to join another organization. We think he's a believer!

George has a similar experience. With his collateral material, he goes to meetings of a Rotary Club and a local Chamber of Commerce. He arrives late to his first meeting and takes the only open seat available. At first he doesn't think anyone at his table is a potential client. But when he practices his new skill of asking open-ended questions, he finds some people might be future clients after all. He also finds out about a few other organizations where people in small business congregate and some contracting firms that are always looking for high-level finance people. He gets some business cards from people who say they'd meet with him in the next week. That next morning, George invests in a Starbucks card so he can treat people to coffee. He is sold on the value of attending meetings!

For Mei, it is a shift in mindset, in the way she frames the whole experience. She has to decide what she really wants to get out of these meetings. She realizes that a good first step would be to meet some friendly contacts who share her interests. So she puts aside all thought of trying to impress people and focuses just on getting to know them. If people ask about her, she gives a brief response and then focuses back on them. Very quickly she realizes that people really like talking about themselves, and if she can just get them talking, she can relax. And she figures out pretty quickly who likes to talk about the stuff she likes to talk about. She starts to build some real relationships. Before long, she's making introductions. Soon people know who she is and see her as a helpful resource. Not a bad position to be in! It took some time, but now the association chapter has become a significant community for her.

Our friends all learned that while approaching meetings requires some strategy, it turns out to be a valuable way to initiate relationships and a terrific way to keep fresh and current in your field.

TAKE ACTION TO POWER YOUR CAREER

Take advantage of routine meetings (whether you like them), and participate in group meetings to learn and enlarge your circle of contacts.

- Before going to a meeting—routine or otherwise—prepare so you can connect with people you'd like to meet or deepen relationships.
- Practice the art of conversation, asking open-ended questions and listening to people's stories. Create some stock conversation-starter questions so you never feel unprepared.
- After the meeting or conference, follow up with those you've met. You can do this via phone, e-mail, LinkedIn, or other social media as well as in face-to-face meetings when it seems wise.

CHAPTER 10

PROMOTE YOUR TEAM AND YOUR DEPARTMENT

Good leadership isn't about advancing yourself. It's about advancing your team.

—John C. Maxwell

Whether you're a department leader, a team leader, or a team member, it helps to be associated with an organization that has a good reputation. Henry, our IT job seeker, is more marketable because he came from a well-reputed firm. The same is true for teams. People judge us in the context of our connections. Your personal brand gets polished, or tarnished, based on your associations—organizations, departments, and even people. So no matter what your role, it is important to promote those around you. It must of course be sincere (you know, the whole "be worthy" thing). If you're a team member, you will be remembered as a positive and generous coworker if you promote the team. If you are the manager or department head, your team will be more loyal, and your reputation will be more broadly established.

Natasha had a wake-up call recently that made her pay more attention to promoting her team. Natasha is successfully building her network with company executives and is also cultivating relationships with some local leaders at other companies. When meeting with Mike, a marketing executive at Prytheon, she runs into Francesca, a former employee of hers. Natasha didn't know that Francesca worked at Prytheon. They had a warm interaction and vowed to connect on LinkedIn.

But Natasha doesn't really know what Francesca might say about her; she realizes Francesca could have real impact on her reputation. Seeing Francesca got Natasha thinking that perhaps her own staff may be feeling a little neglected. Natasha has worked hard on promoting her own reputation, but now she decides to pay at least as much attention to the people who work for her as to those up the chain. People will judge Natasha's reputation not only on how her superiors talk about her but also on their encounters with her staff members.

Natasha decides to be a better leader. She starts bringing Chet, a key manager of hers, to certain high-level presentations and eventually lets Chet present on his own. Chet feels more valued, works harder, and starts getting some visibility for his skills. At the same time, Natasha's reputation grows.

Your reputation and the opportunities that come your way are often intertwined with your team's reputation. You benefit when your department is viewed in a positive light. So how do you cultivate a reputation for your department? Many of the techniques we've discussed in this book are relevant. But in this chapter, we'll share some specific actions you can take, particularly if you're a leader, to elevate the visibility of individuals and the group as a whole. Certainly, once you enter the ranks of leadership, you can't ignore the importance of applying tactful self-promotion to your organization as well as yourself.

Your reputation and the opportunities that come your way are often intertwined with your team's reputation.

Leading a department with a positive reputation yields benefits beyond simply enhancing your own reputation. People want to work in departments with great reputations and for leaders who support their staffs. So the way your department is viewed will affect the kind of people you recruit. If you create a department that can attract top talent, your job becomes easier, and you'll deliver better results. And that spells success for you and the organization.

People want to work in departments with great reputations and for leaders who support their staffs.

Here are a few ideas for promoting your department and staff.

Craft a Department Value Proposition

What value does your department offer the company? Create a statement summarizing the answer, just as you created one for yourself. You might work with your team to develop this statement, which can build team spirit, enthusiasm, and commitment. Each member of the team can then practice his or her own way of delivering the message, so everyone is prepared when asked where they work and what they do. Your team can help spread the message if they know what it is and truly buy into it.

Natasha takes a direct approach. At a staff meeting, she starts a discussion about the department's value proposition. They talk about what customers need most from the department and then explore ideas. Some of the ideas in the mix include, "We breathe life into old products and bring visibility to new ones," "We beat competition to the market," "We produce kick-ass marketing campaigns that clobber the competition," and simply "Great Marketers, Great Partners, Great Results." All are good ideas to play with.

Although not the boss, Mei starts a discussion in her department, and they come up with several options: "We treat employees as well as our best customers," "We help management make this one of the best places to work," and "We put the *human* in human resources." This discussion alone makes a difference in how they view their role in the company. They are optimistic that a value statement can elevate the reputation not only of their area but of the whole HR department.

Once you have a stake in the ground about what your department stands for and delivers, help your team members craft their own value propositions, tied to that of the department. Both your personal reputation and your department's will be shaped by the interactions others have with your staff. It is in your best interests to have your staff members ready to articulate the department's value as well as how they help fulfill that promise.

Support Your Staff in Tactful Self-Promotion

When your staff members interact with executives, attend conferences, or present to other teams in the organization, it elevates your department and your own personal reputation. If you help your team members craft their self-promotion plans and move toward their professional goals, you will reap the rewards in terms of loyalty, engagement, and reputation.

If you help your team members craft their self-promotion plans and move toward their professional goals, you will reap the rewards in terms of loyalty, engagement, and reputation.

Get to know each staff person individually. Depending on how many direct reports you have, take each one to lunch once or twice a year—not linked to a performance review or project, but just to get to know each better. Have wide-ranging discussions and share some of your own life with them. This will build trust and help you get to know them better, which therefore will help you support them to achieve their goals.

Learn their goals and help them succeed. Using what you've learned here, guide staff in determining how they want to be seen and how that reputation will support their goals. Help them come up with some habits and projects that will create the reputation they desire. Of course, you'll need to be candid about their strengths and areas needing development, ensuring they really deserve that reputation. But few things go as far as showing your staff you care about their personal success, not just their ability to deliver the numbers you require.

A HUMBLE IDEA FOR SUPPORTING YOUR EMPLOYEES

If the ideas in this book have worked for you, consider distributing copies to your staff—it saves you time and gives all of you a common vocabulary. Consider discussing the book or a chapter at your ongoing meetings or at a separate monthly lunch. It needn't take a lot of time, but you can use it to help your staff focus on their careers and encourage them to take action. Share some of your actions so they see how it's done and what impact it can have. Working together creates accountability and support that can boost everyone's career.

Give Your Team Exposure and Visibility

One of the most valuable things you can do as a leader is provide opportunities for your staff to gain exposure to key stakeholders (key to their effectiveness in their jobs as well as their future opportunities). This can be paired with giving them the chance to build skills that position them for the future opportunities they seek. Here are some ideas:

- Take a staff person with you to your next professional association or trade meeting. Introduce him or her to leaders in other companies and demonstrate how to work a room. Help your staff make connections that will be good for their careers.

- Give your key people plum assignments so they have chances to grow and shine. People need opportunities to work on something substantial, something that will make a difference. If you offer these opportunities to your staff and coach them toward success, they will sing your praises, and their success will reflect on you as well as your department.
- Recommend your people for good jobs within the company. Call the hiring manager on their behalf. Yes, you may lose a great talent in your department, but you'll keep the talent in the company, and you'll have another advocate in the system. This is yet another place where focusing on others' best interests deepens relationships and pays off in ways you can't imagine.
- Find opportunities for staff people to speak to groups, either internally or externally. It could be about your department or a professional topic. If you know a staff person who is an expert in an area, or is striving to be, find a place for him or her to present.
- If you are asked to speak to a group inside your organization or at an association meeting, consider partnering with a staff person to give him or her a chance to be seen. If the staff member does well—and he or she will, with your coaching—you'll look even better than if you had done it on your own.
- Invite a top executive to your department meeting to discuss where the company is going and answer staff questions (or for whatever purpose makes sense). This will give your team access to a decision maker. If they ask good questions and comport themselves well, they can initiate a relationship, and the executive will leave with a positive view of you and your team.
- If a staff member reports a particularly positive encounter with another leader or a team member in another group (perhaps after a presentation or while on a task force), take the time to write a note sharing the good report with that

person. This reinforces your relationship with the other person and also ensures he or she knows your staff member—all while creating a positive feeling about your staff.

- When you network with other leaders in the organization, don't hesitate to brag a bit about your staff, by name. If one of your staff members or colleagues has been involved in a companywide initiative, brag about his or her success rather than your own. (And while you're at it, if you've heard good things about the other leaders' teams, share it with them too.)
- Also when meeting with other leaders, find out what your staff can do to support them. This uses many of the networking strategies we discussed in earlier chapters, but here you are listening for what your department or staff can do—not just what you personally can do—to add value to and strengthen a relationship.
- When involved in succession planning, be an advocate for your team members. Articulate their value and skills, and make sure their names come up in the conversations that matter.

Review Your Departmental Communications for Consistent Branding

Step back and review every way in which your department communicates what it does inside the organization. If you have an opportunity to feature your group on the company intranet, take the time to shape something that stresses your team's value. Make sure the content is clear and compelling.

If you don't have a newsletter or regular communication shared organization-wide, consider starting one. Make it a developmental assignment for a staff person who would enjoy the task. Share information relevant to your audience. Ensure it is well written. Consider highlighting a staff person each month as a way of promoting both the department and your staff, and have your staff write articles highlighting their expertise.

Assess your department's e-mail signature, if you have control over it. Mei is starting to think like a leader, so she talks with her boss about creating a tagline for their area of HR—something such as "Helping our employees feel good about their jobs." Natasha is thinking of crafting a new departmental signature once she completes their value proposition.

Review your communication protocols (answering phones, e-mail etiquette, etc.). If you really want to build a reputation for your department or area, communications from your team must send the messages you want to be sent. Your stakeholders assess you and your department primarily on their interactions with your people. Make sure everyone on your team sends the right message when they interact with others. Evaluate the following:

Make sure everyone on your team sends the right message when they interact with others.

- How do people answer the phone? A standard greeting can make sure callers have a good experience when connecting with your staff.
- Listen to the voicemail message callers hear when they contact your department or group. Does it align with how you want your area to be seen?
- Set high standards for communications from your staff to stakeholders. For example, expect everyone in your area to write clearly and concisely, with as much personality as is appropriate. Do not allow the use of abbreviations such as LOL, BTW, or OMG. Of course, there are no universal standards because different cultures have different expectations. But you want to send a consistent message about what people can expect from your department and your team. If members of your staff send vague or ambiguous e-mails with misspelled words, that can reflect badly on you and your whole department as well as the individual.

- Help your staff differentiate between what is appropriate for formal and informal written correspondence. This is becoming more complex as texting becomes an accepted form of communication, even with customers. Setting boundaries and educating your staff is part of shaping a culture that sends a consistent message to stakeholders—a message you want to send.

Please don't misunderstand us. We are not fans of regimented communication. We've worked in places where you got your hand slapped if you didn't use the PowerPoint template the corporate office provided. We didn't like it, and we don't expect anyone else does either. However, it is useful to have standards and to expect them to be met. It's a leader's job to establish these guidelines and make sure people know why they are important. Discuss with your team the need for consistent standards of communication so they know why you have set those standards and how they can meet them.

Anyone in the hierarchy can implement most of these suggestions in some measure. You don't have to be a manager to talk up your department and your colleagues. Actually, this type of behavior might well get you into a leadership role more quickly.

In fact, you don't even have to be an employee to advocate for others. Neither George nor Henry is currently working in a traditional job, and yet both find ways to promote others. In a meeting, Henry hears about a job opening that sounds very interesting but not quite right for him. He thinks it might be a great fit for a friend, however, so he talks that person up. His friend really appreciates the advocacy. George, similarly, talks with a company that isn't a good fit for his consulting services, but he recommends another consultant—a "competitor"—and sings her praises to the potential customer. It's a three-way win! The company solves its problem, the other consultant lands a new client, and George's reputation grows.

TAKE ACTION TO POWER YOUR CAREER

Promoting others' accomplishments, elevating your team's visibility, and supporting others' development not only helps others and the organization but also elevates your own reputation.

- Get to know members of your staff or department: What are their goals, what motivates them, what kinds of development opportunities do they need, and with whom do they need to build relationships?
- Find ways to give your employees visibility with leaders who might be influential in their careers.
- Develop consistent communication about what your department stands for—from brand statement to e-mail protocol.

CHAPTER 11

LEVERAGE LINKEDIN AND SOCIAL MEDIA

How to use social media to advance your career is the wrong question. Think instead about advancing the cause, the company, or the profession.

—Rosabeth Moss Kanter

What's your GQ? That is, your Google Quotient. This is essentially what shows up when you google your name. Are you on page one? Is what you find flattering? This is one measure of the success of your online brand. You can have some control over what shows up. George, Natasha, Henry, and Mei all realize they need to make better use of social media to promote their personal brands, to increase their visibility, and to be seen as experts in their fields. Much value can come from a solid social media strategy. But your strategy needs to include more than just what you say about yourself in your LinkedIn profile. In fact, the way you behave on social media will communicate as much about you as the actual words you type—maybe more. Rosabeth Moss Kanter is right in the quote above: like networking, social media should be viewed more as a way to give than to get.

You will present yourself professionally, of course. But your engagement with others on LinkedIn as well as other social sites should focus more on making a contribution than on getting something from others. If you first focus on adding value to your organization, profession, or industry, then you can create the kind of footprint that also serves your personal interests well. You'll be seen as an expert and as a contributor to others' success. If you're seen this way, then when you ask for help—with an introduction, a job search, to promote a book or seminar—your network will likely respond with enthusiasm.

Your engagement with others on LinkedIn as well as other social sites should focus more on making a contribution than on getting something from others.

It's easy to get overwhelmed with all the advice about what to do with which platform: LinkedIn, Facebook, Twitter, Google+, Pinterest, Tumblr, Instagram, and even YouTube! Which of these are necessary, which are optional, and what should you focus on first? Do you have to tweet? And how can you possibly manage all that and still do anything else?

We'll simplify things for you: until you have created a robust LinkedIn profile and enlisted most of your contacts to connect with you on LinkedIn, focus on only this one tool. It is the major platform for professional networking, and if you aren't using it regularly, then you are likely missing out on opportunities. Other sites are optional (unless, of course, they are part of your profession or you enjoy them, in which case we'll discuss how to make them work for you). We'll hit some highlights about your overall social media strategy before zeroing in on LinkedIn. Then we'll provide an overview of how other sites might be useful, depending on your goals.

SOCIAL MEDIA STRATEGY

Just thinking about social media can be overwhelming, much less trying to figure out how to use it to leverage your personal brand. Start by getting a strategic view and determining what you want to get out of your social media activities. Eventually, you'll want to systematize your activities to produce a consistent presence across your media properties (as they are now called). We'll focus on the use of social media to support your career goals.

Assess Your Google Quotient

Check yourself out on Google (and Bing and Yahoo if you like) to see what comes up if your name is searched. If you don't show up at all, then you have some work to do. With a little effort, you can get your LinkedIn profile to page one. You may be able to do the same for some of your other social media sites (such as Google+, or your own website for your consulting practice, or blog posts or articles). But before doing any of that, you need to see where you stand.

When Henry searched for his name, not even his LinkedIn profile showed up on the first few pages. He had no articles or references in the media. He was nowhere to be seen. He figured he had some work to do.

Clean Up Any Negative Content

If someone searching your name is likely to find something embarrassing or damaging, then you may need to do some more aggressive online reputation management. Part of the solution is getting new content out there to push damaging content to later pages. This is a pretty advanced technique, but you can learn to do it, and there are companies that can help. Check the resources section of our website for links to helpful content and services regarding online reputation management.

Be Thoughtful about What You Post

Think about what you post: before you hit send, stop to make sure it aligns with who you are and how you want to be seen as a person and a professional. Nearly everything you put online is discoverable, meaning it can be found. Certainly you want to avoid things that might be really embarrassing. But it's more important to post meaningful content, consistently. Some people post links to articles or some motivational sayings; others post their own daily or weekly thoughts. Others like to jump into forums and comment, answer questions, encourage others. Before you participate in the dialogue, think about how you can best add value to your community—something for which you'd like to stand.

Before you participate in the dialogue, think about how you can best add value to your community—something for which you'd like to stand.

Build a Consistent Brand across All Your Sites

Present a consistent brand as people engage with you in different places. When they interact with you on Facebook, read a tweet, see a LinkedIn update, or see your picture on whatever the most popular site is at the moment, you want the same themes to emerge. Generally it's easiest—and very effective—to use one photo on all your social media profiles. Your content should also be aligned, but not necessarily identical. This would be a good time to look through your positioning statement and your accomplishments and use them to craft your social media messages. Consider the aesthetic, content, and tone of everything that is discoverable about you. If you have influence on it, make sure it's sending the message you want your professional audience to hear.

Take Your Time to Grow Your Social Media Footprint

Don't worry; you're not behind. If you're reading this, you're way ahead of most people. You understand branding, have a point of view or message to communicate, and haven't made a bunch of mistakes (such as posting that photo of yourself doing shots in your underwear—and if you did, you have some repair work to do).

When focused on social media for professional purposes, don't just do anything and everything to get visible. Rather, do the things that will have the greatest impact. So start with one focus—we recommend establishing a terrific LinkedIn profile. Once that is polished, then perhaps you can start sharing articles on LinkedIn, or you can experiment with Twitter or some other platform. But for now, you're just getting started. Build a solid foundation, one brick at a time, starting with LinkedIn.

LEVERAGE LINKEDIN

Love it or hate it, LinkedIn is now an essential tool for managing your career. You may want to use other social media sites, but none is as essential for career success as LinkedIn. It plays into your self-promotion plan in a couple of ways: it showcases and promotes your personal brand, and it gives you a tool for developing and managing your network.

Love it or hate it, LinkedIn is now an essential tool for managing your career.

On this first point, you want to be found by people in need of your kind of talent. A great profile can enhance your visibility inside your company and help position you to secure new roles or assignments (even promotions), and it can help you get noticed by outside recruiters seeking top talent. Second, LinkedIn is a terrific tool for managing your own network by maintaining relationships and visibility. We'll share strategies to grow your network and maintain those relationships so your contacts are accessible and ready to help you when you need it. LinkedIn is also a terrific platform on which to establish yourself as an expert, particularly through publishing articles and commenting on articles by other influencers on the site. We'll cover more about this strategy in the next chapter, when we talk about how to become seen as a thought leader.

The following tips will help you get the most out of the features LinkedIn offers.

Manage Your Invitations

Whom should you invite into your network? We recommend getting to know your contacts before adding them as connections; they are a reflection of who you are professionally. And really, why bother having people in your network that you don't know? If one of your advocates asked for an introduction to someone you added to your LinkedIn network but whom you don't actually know, what would you say? Yes, we know there are differing opinions on this, but relationships are still the keys that open doors for people's careers, and connections you do not know have very little value. On the other hand, you don't need to be too picky about whom you link with. You needn't be close friends or have known someone for a long time, and they don't need to be people just in your profession or even your professional life. Strive for a broad network on LinkedIn.

Instead of using the generic invitation LinkedIn offers, please send a personal message when inviting others to link with you.

There are several ways to grow and engage your LinkedIn network. First, reach out quickly after meeting a new contact, ideally within twenty-four hours, with an invitation to connect. Keep the connection alive; don't let the memory of your initial encounter to fade.

Instead of using the generic invitation LinkedIn offers, *please* send a personal message when inviting others to link with you. This is best done from the person's profile; connecting through an app will send only the generic message and does not allow you to personalize it (at least as of this writing). Comment on your relationship and why you'd like to have the person in your network.

When Henry first started inviting people into his network, he shared that he was looking for work and wanting to connect to discuss his job search. But he jumped the gun. The invitation has one purpose: to motivate the other person to respond with a yes! If you want to get together for coffee, set up a meeting, or set any other agenda, wait! You can follow up after he or she accepts your invitation.

Also personalize your message when accepting a LinkedIn invitation. Yes, you can just click "Accept" and be connected. But take the extra step and send a note about how happy you are to reconnect. This takes only a minute, but believe us, it will pay off dramatically in terms of people feeling connected to you.

Before You Build Your Profile

Review your privacy (and other) settings. Before you renovate your LinkedIn profile, turn off the updates feature so your network won't be inundated with updates about every little thing you change. Review the other settings, especially privacy settings, to make sure you are comfortable with what you are revealing and to whom. There are lots of options in the settings area, so take thirty minutes to become familiar with the options available to you.

Customize your public profile URL. The URL (that is, the uniform resource locator, or web address) for your LinkedIn profile should be customized. When you sign up for an account, you are assigned a profile address made up of random letters and numbers after your name. You can edit it to replace this unmemorable string of characters with your name, thereby strengthening your personal brand. If yours is a common name and has already been claimed by someone else, some tactics for customization include adding your middle initial or name, your academic credentials or profession, or listing your last name first. Or add your location (state or country).

Your final address should look something like www.linkedin.com/in/jilldoe, instead of www.linkedin.com/in/ending with /jill-doe.03dgf58. Once your LinkedIn profile is robust, add this custom URL to your résumé and business cards, and include it in the signature of your e-mails to make it easy for people to visit. This is particularly important for consultants and job seekers.

Be keyword aware. Know the keywords for your profession and the searches you want to show up in. How might recruiters search for people like you? First you have to find these words, and then you must use them strategically in your profile. One strategy for finding keywords is to review other people's LinkedIn profiles. Find people positioning themselves similarly and see what they stress. Review their summary and skills sections and take notes. If you want to position yourself for more responsibility, you might also see how people a level up position themselves and what keywords they use.

If you want to position yourself for more responsibility, you might also see how people a level up position themselves and what keywords they use.

Henry takes a systematic look at the job postings that interested him most. He does it the old-fashioned way, printing copies of a few postings and using a highlighter to identify specific words and phrases that seem important. When he looks through his highlighted words, some themes surprise him. For example, *team-oriented* and *collaborative* are mentioned in all of them. He decides he better make sure these words (which are true of him) appear in his profile more prominently.

Similarly, George goes to his competitors' LinkedIn profiles and websites to see how they position themselves and what words they emphasize. After taking some notes, he comes up with a list that includes *finance*, *financial systems*, *ERP*, *systems conversions*, *International Financial Reporting Standards (IFRS)*, *GAAP*, *project leadership*, and *change management.*

Using industry-specific keywords throughout your profile will increase your ranking in searches. Repeating keywords gives them more power in the ranking. The most important fields to focus on are headline, job titles, and summary. These are more heavily weighted, so the right words in these fields will get you the most traction. If you're looking for work, find ways to get the job titles you are seeking into your profile.

Build a Powerful Profile

Your LinkedIn profile is a central communication tool that will be consulted in numerous situations (when someone is looking for an employee or consultant, considering you for a board position, thinking about putting you on a task force or special assignment, etc.). So you need your profile to be effective. The following tips will help you build a powerful profile that will elevate your brand.

Include a photo! Your photo may be the most important part of your profile in terms of attracting attention once you show up in a search. People make assumptions about you based on that photo. It can strengthen relationships with people, giving them a better sense of who you are. If you don't have a photo, people may wonder what you're hiding. Get a professional head shot or have a friend with some skill take one of you. It's wise to look approachable and friendly—someone people would like working with—rather than too formal or serious.

Create a clear and compelling headline. Use a brand description under your name rather than your former or current title (which is the default). Make it keyword rich and focused on what you want to be known for. One of our favorites is from a corporate training leader: Learning that Fits, Learning that Works, Learning that Lasts. Additional examples include:

- Operations Leader—Optimizing Performance through Lean Six Sigma
- Senior Finance Leader | Financial Planning & Analysis | Mergers and Acquisitions
- Innovative Mechanical Engineer who creates great products and great relationships
- Resourceful Executive Assistant who helps make an executive's life run smoothly
- Human Resources Business Partner | Senior Generalist | SPHR | Relationship Builder

If looking for work, avoid using "in transition" or "seeking new opportunity" in your headline.

Craft a summary that expresses your personal brand. Start with the value proposition work you did in the first section of this book. Your summary is precisely this: a value proposition. It should emphasize the same themes as the summary on your résumé. Here are a few tips for producing an excellent summary:

- Describe who you are and how are you unique. What types of outcomes do you produce? What value do you add?
- Keep it focused on the reader. How do you want the reader (e.g., a recruiter, hiring manager, prospective employee, task force leader) to see you?
- Consider writing your profile in the first person. Think of it more as a story you are telling than a list of skills. You have more room in this profile than you generally have on a résumé, so you might as well use the space.
- If you are looking for work, consider including some key accomplishments and company names in the summary. Recruiters may not read past the summary, so make sure you pack in anything that really works to your advantage. Include your contact information here as well.

Make the skills section work for you. Your first step here is to pick the ten keywords or phrases you want to be known for and put them in the top ten slots. Then fill in the rest with other relevant keywords. People can endorse you for particular skills. Take advantage of this feature; reach out and ask people to endorse you. You want at least ten endorsements for each of your top-ten skills. Don't forget to endorse others, always because you mean it. It reinforces relationships, and the activity on LinkedIn will help you boost your profile's rank. And others might just reciprocate.

Highlight outcomes and proof of your brand promise in the experience section. When describing your experience, include a brief statement of responsibility to show the scope of the position, and add a few accomplishments that show outcomes or results. This will help illustrate the themes outlined in your summary.

Expand information in the title section, especially if your title is unusual. Be honest, but include other functional responsibilities a recruiter might search for. This is a similar strategy to what we recommended in your headline. Here are a few examples:

- VP Finance (SEC Reporting | Financial Planning and Analysis)
- Project Manager (Lean Six Sigma | IT Project Implementation)
- Marketing Manager (Market Research | Consumer Insights | Analytics)
- R&D Technician (Electrical | Mechanical | Prototype | Precision Machining)

Add additional sections to your profile. There are many additional sections that you can include in your profile, including certifications, languages, publications, patents, projects, volunteering, and many others. Check them out and see if you have content you might include. Natasha uploads the article she wrote. She is now considering writing something on global marketing (and when she does, she'll certainly highlight it on LinkedIn).

Choose the order in which your profile flows. You can drag sections of your profile and place them in whatever order you choose, so be selective about what follows your summary. For your specific purposes, what follows best? Is it experience, education, publications, skills? Again, you can review the sample profiles on our website for some good examples.

When Mei was just getting started in her job search, trying to move from food service to a corporate HR job, she placed her education section (showing her degree in HR) just after her summary and before experience. She thought this would help her be seen in the right light. Henry adds a section for patents and places it after his experience. As George grows his visibility and publishes an article, he may well choose to put the publication section after the summary to emphasize his expertise in the field. Ultimately, you need to arrange your profile to make the best impression with your target audience.

Consider uploading sample documents. LinkedIn now makes it fairly simple to add video, photos, and other examples of your work to your profile. Visual content is most compelling here, whereas published articles, conference presentations, and similar content can be listed in the publications section. Adding relevant content to your site differentiates you. Pay attention to other profiles to see what leaders in your area are doing in this regard.

George uploads his bio, a one-page overview of his consulting model, and a PowerPoint presentation he put together highlighting some things to be careful about when implementing a new finance system. He believes these items will help readers understand his perspective and see him as more of an expert.

What documents would support your brand? Is there something you can create for this purpose?

Secure Recommendations

There are two ways people can support your skills on LinkedIn. They can endorse your skills and expertise, as described earlier. Or they can write recommendations for a particular position or role from your work history. Recommendations are much more powerful than endorsements. Having some great recommendations can help you stand out and convey information to a reader that you may not want to say yourself (for fear of seeming like a braggart). Recommendations will also help you rank higher in search results because the keywords are embedded and because LinkedIn gives them more weight. The algorithm reads recommendations as "This person has some advocates," so it gives you more. If you want to be found, recommendations will help more than endorsements. And once you are found, they will enhance how the reader sees you.

Having some great recommendations can help you stand out and convey information to a reader that you may not want to say yourself.

So how do you go about securing recommendations? First off, ask for them. Some people might write a recommendation without a request, but it's rare, so reach out to your advocates. Ask in live conversations or e-mail exchanges if they would be willing to write recommendations. The personal touch is a way to both secure solid references and reinforce important relationships. And if they are willing, then you can discuss areas you'd like them to address. You might consider offering to draft the content of the recommendation. Busy people are more likely to say yes if you provide text they can personalize, and it's likely to get done more rapidly.

Ask your advocates to be specific in their descriptions of your value rather than offer general praise. For example, "I really enjoyed working with Joshua—he's a great guy" is not as powerful as "Joshua is a terrific manager—I've never worked harder for anyone." Or "Jessie not only puts together detailed project plans, but she also executes them flawlessly." You want the recommendations to reinforce the themes you articulate in your summary. So it is wise to provide those who are writing recommendations with some bullet points about what you're hoping they can speak to.

Finally, if you want to get recommendations, recommending others is a good strategy. An unsolicited recommendation (delivered without an immediate request for a recommendation in return) is a powerful relationship builder. Make sure your recommendation is sincere.

Join and Engage in LinkedIn Groups

Join groups related to your field, university alumni groups, local and national networking groups, special interest groups. Pick which groups should appear on your public profile. How do you find the right groups to join? You could do what Mei does—she visits the profiles of her peers and those up the ladder to get ideas. This is a great way to find out where people you want to connect with are hanging out.

Posting just twice a week in a couple of groups can make you more visible to others in the group as well as increase your ranking on LinkedIn (which loves people who are active). Make sure your postings are substantial and add to the conversation. You need to post more than "Great idea, John." Acknowledging John's idea is good, of course, because it strengthens relationships, but then your comment should go on to add value to the conversation.

Stay Visible and Active on LinkedIn

LinkedIn is a narcissist. What do we mean by this? Well, it thinks only of itself! If you do something inside the LinkedIn system, it takes notice, it thinks you're cool, and it rewards you by improving your ranking in searches. Basically, once it completes its review of keywords, it looks at your behavior on LinkedIn. If you are active in groups, post updates, have recommendations, and actively recommend others, then LinkedIn considers you to be more active than your peers and puts you higher on the list!

There are lots of ways to stay active in LinkedIn so you become more visible: use the Post an Update feature, follow companies, post content into groups, get recommendations, give recommendations, endorse people, get endorsed, send InMails, invite people into your network, reach out to others to stay in touch, respond to other people's updates, and many more. These activities give your profile an edge.

THE ADVANTAGES OF ENGAGING IN LINKEDIN GROUPS

Why would you want to generate more e-mail to your inbox by joining groups? Executive LinkedIn Coach Carol Kaemmerer—author of the upcoming book *LinkedIn for the Savvy Executive*—explains that becoming a group member has many advantages.

- Your ranking on a keyword search is influenced by your relationship with the person searching. So, it is important to have a robust network, and joining a single group can expand your network by thousands of people.
- You can communicate directly and privately through the group to any member.
- You'll get access to great articles you can share with your connections.
- You may develop online relationships with other members of the group as you participate in discussions.
- The act of participation in group discussions increases your visibility both within the group and with your network.

George makes a habit of finding excellent articles relevant to his target audience, and he sends one to his prospects and customers every two weeks. He also tags each connection—a valuable feature in LinkedIn—so he can send posts and articles to specific groups of connections. This allows him to easily sort for his connections in the IT field, those in management roles in the IT field, and so on, and then he can send notes to just that targeted group.

Keep Learning!

LinkedIn is changing fast, so you need to stay up to date. LinkedIn provides some great resources in its Learning Center. You can also subscribe to the company's blog at http://blog.linkedin.com; this will keep you current on the latest developments. Other books and online resources are outlined at our website. These change regularly, so check www.TactfulSelfPromotion.com for new and updated resources.

BEYOND LINKEDIN

Yes, there are other social media sites that might be useful in your self-promotion arsenal, but none as essential as LinkedIn. With one caveat: if your work includes working with social media or digital marketing, then you may need to be on these other sites to demonstrate your expertise. If you are later in your career and striving to demonstrate that you're a contemporary contributor, not an atrophying older worker, you might want to post on Twitter. So yes, there are uses for these other sites, but they aren't as important for most of our readers as LinkedIn. If you are interested in expanding your digital profile, consider these as additional options.

Facebook

Facebook is the single largest network of people in the world, larger than even a large country! And if networking and connecting with people is important to a career, then connecting with the people who care about you (friends and family) is also part of career success. If you are looking for opportunities (a job, a consulting assignment, a resource to interview, etc.), your Facebook community can be a great place to ask for help. HR professionals and even hiring managers are also beginning to use it to look for more information about people they are considering hiring, assigning to a task force, or granting a consulting assignment. So your profile, what you post, and how you interact with your network could affect your opportunities.

Make sure you take the privacy settings in Facebook seriously. You do have quite a bit of control over who sees your posts—ranging from the entire public, to your friends and their friends, to just your friends, or to even just you. You can create custom groups to which you can post certain types of information. For example, you can post holiday event information and photos only to those who attend, or links of career interest only to professional contacts. Most people don't know their privacy settings. This is an important project to take on so you can be confident you're sharing appropriate information with appropriate audiences.

If a company representative has an interest in you, she or he will find your profile on Facebook. Review your profile to make sure it represents you well to a hiring manager. You don't need to make it a professional, work-focused site; just be thoughtful about what content you post. Know that it will be found and might have an impact on future opportunities. Complete your education and work history sections. Consider including a favorite (publicly appropriate) quote that reveals a point of view. And review your whole profile for writing and grammar. Assume an influencer will read and review it with this in mind.

If, like Henry, you are searching for work, creating a complete profile is particularly important. Henry knows that interested hiring managers will likely find their way to his Facebook page to learn more about him, so he makes sure his profile is complete, his photo is professional (and aligned with his other photos on social media sites), and his header photo is appropriate. Although not work related, the header isn't embarrassing; he chooses a picture of himself and his kids playing in the park. He figures if someone doesn't want to hire him because of his kids, then he doesn't want to waste his time talking with that company.

Before his job search, Henry had only used Facebook to keep in touch with friends and family, just as it was initially designed to do. But now that he's looking for work, he realizes he has access to a large network of people who will likely help him if they know what he's looking for. He decides to be more strategic when using Facebook. First he uses it to research companies he finds interesting by "liking" their corporate Facebook pages. This way he gets updates and lots of links to resources. He also starts posting a few more items about his professional area.

Twitter

People who don't like Twitter complain about the inanity of the culture of tweeters—those who tweet what they have for breakfast, how much they hate traffic or the weather, and so on. But if you're saying something along these lines, then you probably haven't tried Twitter.

Many Twitter users are serious-minded professionals, eager to share their learnings and connect with others.

You may not like it, but it is a powerful form of communication, networking, and information sharing. People on Twitter want to be part of a conversation. It's up to you to determine which conversations to be a part of and which to follow. Many Twitter users are serious-minded professionals, eager to share their learnings and connect with others. For consultants and job seekers, Twitter can be enormously helpful.

Spend a little time evaluating Twitter as a tool and then make an informed decision about your level of involvement. If you are social and like connecting with people and ideas, then Twitter can work as an extension of your already gregarious nature. Many introverts also love Twitter and are brilliant at using it to connect with others.

You don't need to jump into Twitter with both feet. Twitter can be an invaluable research tool, something you can happily use every day without sending a single tweet. Once you join Twitter, you can follow a few thought leaders in your field.

This is how George sticks his foot in. He decides to take a peek and poke around for a few minutes to see how it works. He starts following a couple of popular financial writers, and they post some very current information. He realizes that not everyone tweets about their lunches; many are staying in touch with emerging trends. He sees that by following specific companies and leaders, he can stay ahead of the curve and stay relevant. As he gets more comfortable, maybe he will start to put himself out there and send a tweet or two.

Additional Social Media Sites

In addition to LinkedIn, Facebook, and Twitter, there are many other social media sites, some focused broadly and others focused on specific disciplines or niches. Some of the most popular sites include Google+, Pinterest, Tumblr, Instagram, Flickr, Vine, and Pheed—and there are new ones every day! Keep your eyes open, and ask savvy people where they find value. Also note that many organizations have a company intranet sharing site that may be valuable to you.

Check out a new site every couple of months and determine whether it makes sense to have a presence there. Again, there are a lot of sites, and they change all the time, so you should be deliberate about where you show up. Review your social media strategy quarterly and see where you find the most value.

MANAGING YOUR SOCIAL MEDIA ACTIVITIES

With all this activity in social media, you need to keep your eyes on what's happening. And you have to establish a routine. Make a simple list of things you can do each week to manage your social media activity and then schedule time to do them. Individually, each task takes only a minute, a few at most. But they are easy to ignore or forget because they are not urgent. If you want to really establish yourself in your career, establishing your online brand and keeping it alive is an urgent task. So schedule it in. There's no need to do more than twenty minutes of social media stuff at a time. It's the cumulative effect that pays off. You want to feed the beast a little at a time, sending some fuel into it every day or two, through different channels.

You can certainly manage your own social media, particularly if it interests you. But it can be cumbersome. The good news is that now there are many good tools available to help you manage your social media presence. These tools can save you a lot of time by providing a single dashboard that lets you see and act on all your social media sites. You can schedule a week's worth of posts to go out at times you specify. Set it up once, and the week is done. Of course, you can also perform impulse posts. But even if you're a super-tweeter who stays very active, you can still benefit from systematizing some of your messaging. Planning it out at least a week ahead ensures that you think through your plan for staying visible for the right reasons. Because this area changes quickly, we won't name names here for these management tools, but please check out our website for fresh resources.

If you want to really establish yourself in your career, establishing your online brand and keeping it alive is an urgent task.

There is so much information out there about using social media to further your career. Had we not been rigorous in our focus, we could have written this book about that topic alone. But if you decide to make social media a serious part of your career plan, or if you are in job search (in which case you *must* leverage social media), we recommend one book that covers all the basics: *Job Searching with Social Media for Dummies,* by our colleague Joshua Waldman. Although it focuses on job search, almost everything in it is relevant for elevating a personal brand. It covers many more strategies and offers some detailed discussions of how to execute these strategies. It is well worth the read.

TAKE ACTION TO POWER YOUR CAREER

Social media is just a part of our lives; it casts an ongoing story about us that shapes, in some measure, how we're seen by others. We can help shape that narrative in a direction that supports our goals. It's worth the effort to build some good habits around your use of social media.

- Clean up your social media mess (if you have one). If any embarrassing photos or stories show up when people search for your name, do what you can to replace that content with new content, or work with a professional service to minimize its impact.
- Pick your platforms and build consistent messaging. Use LinkedIn as your core social media site and then expand to other sites, as you choose.
- Engage with your colleagues and friends. Use social media for its intended purpose—connecting with and helping others—rather than just to project your brand into the world. This is what will make social media pay off for you.

CHAPTER 12

BE SEEN AS A THOUGHT LEADER

Example is not the main thing in influencing others, it is the only thing.

—Albert Schweitzer

Who has the edge—the generalist or the expert? Today you need to be both broad and deep: general skills are required but expertise is valued (and rewarded). When you're viewed as an expert in your field, you are more likely to be recruited to bigger jobs, sought out to solve the more interesting problems, or weigh in on decisions in which your expertise is required. By sharing your expertise, you become a resource to others, which helps you build relationships. Think about how much further ahead George or Natasha would be if they had worked on being seen as experts in their fields. And yes, it takes work, but the opportunity is there and much more available than people imagine.

By sharing your expertise, you become a resource to others, which helps you build relationships.

So how do you become seen as an expert? If you're earlier in your career, your first step might be to become the go-to person in your department, as someone willing and able to help with specific issues. If you are more established in your career, then you can move to some other common paths: speaking, blogging, writing articles, publishing books, and becoming a voice in the media. Each strategy can establish you as a thought leader and help elevate your visibility on the local scene or even on the national or international stage. To get ahead in your career, you do not *need* to do these things, but they help. And for some people (like George, who is trying to build his consulting practice), it may be critical.

For some people, contemplating how to become a thought leader can take some wind out of their sails. If you can't quite see yourself doing these things, stick with us: we think you'll find that some of these strategies are much more doable, and less intimidating, than you may think.

You may have noticed that we do not define a *thought leader* here as "one who wrote the book that revolutionized a new profession or created a new paradigm." There's no need to be *the* expert in the field. Rather, you can start by becoming known for a more specific expertise. Pick something you are good at and enjoy sharing with others, and focus on that. For example, Henry might focus on Cloud technology, his favorite IT trend. Natasha might pick a particular international region and become knowledgeable about how to penetrate that particular space. Don't strive to be original; strive to be *useful*. Start by thinking about what you know that could really help people in your organization or profession. Pick a specific niche, and focus your attention there.

Now let's get into some of the strategies.

CURATING OTHERS' CONTENT FOR SOCIAL MEDIA

This strategy is relatively easy to implement. When you see an article in your area of expertise, "curate" it. That is, comment on the specific points you like, or note why it is interesting, and then post it on LinkedIn or other social media. When you consistently provide access to carefully chosen articles with helpful commentary, people will recognize you as a subject-matter expert. To find content worthy of curating, set up some Google Alerts for your chosen topics and watch your LinkedIn groups for articles on point. Identify and follow other experts in your area, and share their content with attribution—but include your own commentary. By aligning yourself with experts who consistently provide good content, your "likes, comments, and shares" will help you become known as someone knowledgeable about the same area.

When you consistently provide access to carefully chosen articles with helpful commentary, people will recognize you as a subject-matter expert.

And because you are consistently curating the best articles in your area of expertise, you may develop the confidence to take the next steps: writing and speaking.

WRITING ARTICLES

Writing articles on targeted topics can be an easy way to get more visibility in the larger professional community. This doesn't have to be a big or complicated project.

Don't Be Intimidated—Just Get Started

Take a look at the PTA newsletter, your company newsletter, or the local chapter of your professional association, and write an article for it. Keep it short—three paragraphs. Offer tips or tricks ("Six Ways to . . ." or "Five Tips for . . ."), or write a little news story (who, what, when, where, why). Report on a conference or review a book. Simply offer a perspective on a topic you care about, one relevant to your audience and aligned with how you want to be seen.

Don't worry about being original. The most popular articles generally don't reveal anything new about a topic. Instead, they convey a few good ideas in an interesting way. They may include some examples people haven't heard before, but rarely are they radical, new thoughts. We know this from our own writing. For example, if we were to write an article on LinkedIn, we would offer seven tips for creating a powerful profile. But we bet *you* could write that same article after reading three or four other articles on the topic, and it would probably be on point! Just pick a topic of interest to you and to those with influence in your company, profession, or industry.

Simply offer a perspective on a topic you care about, one relevant to your audience and aligned with how you want to be seen.

And don't worry about the technical aspect of posting your article. LinkedIn provides an exceptionally easy-to-use platform for your content (long-form posts). Search for a commercially available image to illustrate your article, think of a clever headline, write your text—then upload it to their platform.

Brainstorm a Variety of Topics

You may recall from chapter 8 that Natasha wrote an article that required her to interview senior leaders (thereby broadening strategic relationships). She chose that article topic very strategically after brainstorming with a couple of colleagues and then running some options past her boss. She felt her preparation paid off with a compelling article and the opportunity to connect with senior leaders.

Come up with three or four topics that are useful to your audience and relevant to how you want to be known. Share your list of ideas with a few colleagues to see which they think might be the most interesting or useful.

Google the topics that interest you to see what others are writing. If some topics have a million articles, don't shy away because you think everything's already been said. It hasn't been said by you yet. And if the topic is that popular, it's a space you probably want to be seen in.

Target Publications

Which publications (online or offline) should you approach? You don't have to pick the national magazine for your professional association. You could instead focus on your local chapter's newsletter. They always need content, and you're more likely to be seen by your local colleagues in this venue. Of course, if you are positioning yourself as a national figure, then a national publication would be worth pursuing—but it isn't necessary. In addition to professional association newsletters, take a look at journals, magazines, e-zines, newspapers, popular websites and blogs, and so on. Perhaps your departmental or company newsletter or intranet site would be the best place for your content. There's no need to be too ambitious to get the impact you desire. Just pick a few places where your topic might be of interest and reach out.

Tap into Resources to Produce Your Article

You don't need to do everything yourself, and there are plenty of resources available to help you write an article.

- Interview people to gather current data. This also gives you an opportunity to meet people and increase your visibility, as Natasha did for her article.
- Find a coauthor. This can be fun and motivating, not to mention an opportunity to deepen connections with someone in your field.
- If you're concerned about your writing skills or if you want your article to be especially polished, connect with a professional writer or editor.

- For writing tips, one great resource is copyblogger.com. They have tons of free content on everything from crafting powerful headlines, to researching topics, to structuring an article, to understanding the whole craft of writing, especially for the web. If you visit the site, set a time limit—you'll get sucked in. But it's worth the risk!

Once he knows he wants to write an article, George conducts an informal poll of his former colleagues and prospective customers to find out what topics they'd like more information about, as well as which publications they read most often and respect. He gets some help from a professional writer and creates two articles on current issues in financial systems. Then he reaches out to some key publications and asks if he could submit his articles, and now he's a published writer!

Approach the Publications

Actually, you don't even need to approach publications anymore. You can publish an article on LinkedIn, a feature that used to be exclusive but has now opened up to everyone. Like most readers, we tend to assume an article is more credible if it is first published in a professional association newsletter, journal, magazine, or other third-party publication. But a few timely and frequently shared articles on LinkedIn can build your Google Quotient and even entice other publications to take you on.

Consider Creating an Infographic

The world is quickly becoming focused on images and not narrative. You can use this trend to your advantage and create an infographic rather than a long-form text. An infographic is simply a visual picture of information. Search Google for "best infographics," and you'll get a slew of samples. Some of them are very elaborate, but others are quite simple. And of course, you don't have to create these yourself. Once you have the content, you can hire a professional to create the infographic for a very reasonable rate. Visit elance.com or fiverr.com, and you'll find talented designers eager to work for you.

Leverage the Article

Once the article is published, your work is not done. You want to draw attention to it. Here are a few ideas.

- Post it on your LinkedIn profile, on your website and blog (if you have them), and on any social media sites you operate.
- Create a post with a link to the article on your Facebook page, especially if you have a lot of professional friends on Facebook. You might even spend a few dollars promoting the post to make sure more people see it.
- Post links to the article in relevant LinkedIn group discussions and other blogs (and have your friends do the same).
- Send it out to your network with enthusiasm: "This article just got published in XYZ. I'm excited to share it with you!" Would you be offended if one of your contacts alerted you to an article he or she had written, especially if the topic was in your field? Probably not—most people will think it's cool!
- Make copies and bring it to job interviews as an example of your interest in and commitment to the field. Better yet, mention it when appropriate and send the article along with your follow-up note.
- List it as a publication on your résumé.

Publishing articles is a great strategy if you are pursuing a career change of any kind. Pick a topic related to the new field. Read a couple of books, sift through some articles and blogs, and interview a few people about the topic of interest. Then write about it. Your byline on an article related to the new field will demonstrate a commitment and will position you as a thought leader in this particular area.

Our Friends Go to Press!

After her initial success with her in-house article, Natasha focuses on writing an article on trends in global marketing. This is a good choice because even though she doesn't have a lot of international experience, she wants to be known in this area. She decides to use the article as a reason to reach out to some global marketing leaders in her field so they can discuss general trends, help her focus on a topic, and identify content for her article. Who knows—some of these folks might become her mentors or employers, or both. Natasha's approach integrates her need to build a network in the global space and to become known by some movers and shakers. In addition, it also gives her a piece of collateral material (the article) to promote.

Natasha's project demonstrates a favorite strategy of ours: integrating multiple actions toward the same goal. Creating a larger project such as an article accomplishes a variety of things at once, all of which support your goals. In this case, Natasha gains knowledge by researching a topic of interest, builds relationships with key people, and positions herself as a thought leader in the space where she wants to play. And it's fun for her! She finds that it's easier to reach out to people to discuss trends in support of an article than to reach out for general networking purposes. The article gives her the entrée she needs to initiate relationships.

PUBLIC SPEAKING

There's no denying that speaking at events and presenting at meetings are terrific ways to get out there and be visible. Like all of our other techniques, public speaking adds value by providing useful, relevant information to people interested in the things you know.

Start Where You Feel Comfortable

You don't have to start by delivering a keynote address. Henry is afraid of public speaking, but he wants to be more visible. So he joins a committee in his professional association and gets involved in researching and securing speakers for the events. This turns out to be a terrific networking opportunity.

Henry takes on the task of introducing each speaker before the presentation, which makes him visible and associates him with leaders in his field—all without him having to be a speaker himself. He's nervous enough about his first introduction, but he prepares and does it well. People laugh at his opening joke. He feels good about it and thinks that perhaps he might like speaking after all. In any case, it's great exposure for him. If you are already comfortable presenting to a group, then you might want to take it further than Henry and work up a presentation.

Where Should You Speak?

There are many opportunities to speak. Start by brainstorming places where you might speak, and then target two or three to reach out to and gauge their interest.

You don't need to begin by giving a keynote address at the National Press Club or delivering a TED talk. Instead, start by presenting to audiences that likely make you comfortable, such as to a local nonprofit, school, or church group. These organizations are often pleased to have speakers share their content. The point is to find opportunities to practice.

Don't ignore speaking opportunities inside your company.

Don't ignore speaking opportunities inside your company. Larger companies often have affinity groups that look for speakers on various topics. Check with the training department to see if they could use you as a guest speaker in any of their onboarding or ongoing courses. You can meet a lot of people inside your company by making a few speeches.

Think about where professionals in your field gather: conferences, professional and industry association meetings, service clubs, and so on. Other places to explore include continuing education programs and local colleges and universities. Many professors like to bring members of the professional community into the classroom to provide guest lectures or simply share their experiences of the business world. Check with your local colleges, see what their programs are, and find out if there is a place where you can add value. If you do a guest lecture, put it on your résumé and LinkedIn profile.

For people just getting their feet wet in speaking, joining a local Toastmasters group is a must. This provides weekly practice of spontaneous and prepared presentations in a very supportive, low-risk setting. Check for locations and times, and most importantly, a group of people you enjoy.

This is what Henry decides to do. He has been networking and gathering ideas about the impact of Cloud technology on his area of IT. After joining a Toastmasters group and becoming more comfortable with speaking, he approaches his local professional association and offers to share his recent learnings at one of the group events. He asks for just ten minutes to give an overview. He doesn't need to be the keynote speaker; he'll just share three or four slides and give a couple of examples about what he's learned. He gets the go-ahead! The day of the event, he hands out printed copies of his slides (with his contact information on them, of course). The presentation goes well, and now he's thinking of offering to deliver it elsewhere. He also posted the slides on his LinkedIn profile and sent an update to his network announcing that the materials from his presentation are available to be read and shared. Henry's getting the hang of it.

Panel Discussions

Participating in a panel discussion can be less stressful than carrying an entire speech by yourself. Conferences often host panels; sign up early and volunteer to speak on a topic of interest. You can also volunteer to assemble a panel and serve as the moderator, which means preparing some questions and keeping the conversation going. You get to be at center stage, surrounded by experts, but you don't have to be the expert yourself.

Not long ago, Richard's brother, David, called him and said he wanted to become more visible on the speaker's circuit. He assumed he'd have to start in his local marketplace and work for a couple of years to make it to the big time. Richard asked where David most wanted to speak. David is a restaurant branding consultant (and owns a great cookie factory called The Graceful Cookie), so his target audience congregated at the National Restaurant Association national conference.

After some contemplation, Richard suggested that David "parachute in" to the conference by approaching three of his most well-known clients or business partners and assembling a panel on branding. (Notice the way Richard became an advocate for his brother!) David asked three people with very different points of view (a corporate food-service leader, the head of a firm that designs restaurants, and the leader of restaurants for a series of high-end hotels and conference centers) to join him on the panel. He proposed to craft presentations with each of them, create slides, and tie it all together. They were all flattered, seeing the benefit for themselves of becoming more visible to this audience (and with little work). David crafted a proposal, submitted it to the national conference, and was accepted. He then got to work delivering on his promise. The panel presentation was a great success. David was on stage for ninety minutes with three leaders of his profession, and he moderated—so people thought he must be someone! The next year, David was asked to submit a proposal, and he returned the following year with his own presentation.

David's technique does not have to be used on so bold a scale. Try it for a local association or even your company's affinity group or professional development day. What matters is finding a way to be seen with the right people. You don't need to be a global celebrity: just get a little buzz going among those who matter for your career.

Give It a Try

Many resources can help you prepare presentations and speak in public. Books and blogs are helpful, but nothing helps more than real, live practice, with coaching. If you live in a town with ongoing education programs, see what they offer in the public speaking arena. Check out our website for more resources.

What's important right now is not to let a fear of public speaking drive you away from this excellent vehicle that can add value to your profession and increase your visibility as a thought leader. Start small, as Henry did, by just introducing a speaker. Then perhaps assemble a panel, and maybe offer your own presentation to a group inside your company or local community.

BE A RESOURCE TO THE PRESS

This strategy is particularly important for people who are self-employed or freelancers. If you work in a corporation, check the company policy for talking with the press, or talk with your communications department about appropriate approaches.

Once you start writing articles or a blog, you may decide to make yourself available to the press as a resource. This can include television, radio, magazines, e-zines, newspapers, and podcasts. There is a great need for articulate experts to participate in these ventures; without content, these vehicles die. So you can position yourself to contribute, which allows you to help others while increasing your visibility.

Select the Appropriate Venues to Approach

Keep your audience in mind. You don't need visibility with everyone. *People* magazine might be huge, but it might not reach your key audience. In contrast, a local business journal or trade association newsletter might be much smaller, but it's likely better connected to your audience. Your first step is to research the marketplace and identify which media type would best serve your needs. Make sure to read these publications or watch or listen to these shows, carefully, so you know what type of stories they cover. Pay attention to topics, length, tone, and other presentation factors. You need to craft your approach based on each publication.

Feed the Media What It Eats

The media needs stories. You need to find a way to feed the media, helping the press create stories (and on a deadline). Develop a list of potential stories the media might (or should) cover in your profession or industry. To which of these stories might you contribute? Consider pitching your own story—do you, your department, your company, or your consulting firm have a unique story you think might interest others? If so, write up a brief overview about why it's relevant to their audience, and send it to an editor. If you have something slightly controversial, contrary to the common view, or particularly entertaining or informative, the media may well be interested.

Craft Your Media or Press Kit

The media will want to know who you are and why you're a credible source. Consider creating your own media kit with a biography, articles you've written, press mentions or quotes by or about you, a sample Q&A (for example, an interview), a sample video clip, customer references and testimonials, and so on. If you have your own business or consulting firm, prepare a fact sheet about your business and its story.

Cultivate Relationships with the Media

Finding journalists who cover your area of expertise in isn't all that hard. Who writes about your profession? You're probably reading their work. Online articles often include journalists' e-mail addresses in their bios at the bottom. Message them with specific, real praise about their articles. Do this occasionally, and then when you want to request advice about how to become a source for articles in your space, those journalists will likely respond to you. You can also find journalists on LinkedIn, in which case you'd look for a shared contact and ask for an introduction, or contact them directly with an InMail.

As you interact with the media and offer yourself as an expert, they will expect something from you as well: responsiveness, insight, a brief and cogent perspective, and most importantly, something quotable. If you are looking to be interviewed for radio or in a video format, then you need to prepare yourself. It takes some special training to do that well, so we won't try to cover it here. Just remember: the key is in your preparation. You need to know what stories you want to tell, and you need to be able to tell them in a very abbreviated way (in most cases). There are many resources to help you prepare for these types of events. Check out our website for some links.

Leverage Your Media Appearances

Promote your media appearances, whether in the form of an article, television or radio show, podcast, or other venue. You can do this in a variety of ways. Send an announcement to your network. For example, you can use LinkedIn to target a specific group of your contacts (using tags) and send them a note about it. Or you can send out an update to your entire LinkedIn network with the post updates feature. If appropriate, post it on your LinkedIn profile and other social media sites. If your appearance or contribution is posted somewhere on the Internet, then you can share the link with your comments in relevant LinkedIn groups.

ADDITIONAL STRATEGIES FOR BUILDING AUTHORITY

There are lots of other things you can do to establish yourself as a thought leader. You don't *need* to do these things, but they can be helpful. And for people like George, who is starting his consulting practice, some of these might be essential. Here are more things to consider.

Launch Your Own Website

Having your own website—especially if you can use your name as the domain name (e.g., www.JohnDoe.com)—provides you with a place to organize and share all your relevant content. Most people do this once they start a blog, but you can create a site that simply lets you share your background and history, similar to a résumé. This format also lets you include images, links to other sites of interest, and other evidence supporting your value statement. You can show more of what you want people to see and express more personality than you can in a résumé or on LinkedIn. If you are consulting or have your own business, this will be essential.

The good news is that you no longer need to have technical skills to get a great-looking website. Numerous services offer beautiful templates that let you plug in your content. You will find freshly updated resources for building your own website on our website, in the resources section.

Leverage the Authority of LinkedIn

In the previous chapter, we focused a lot on LinkedIn, particularly how to build a powerful profile. But LinkedIn is also becoming a terrific platform on which to build your authority. Once you've optimized your profile, you can leverage that foundation to build authority. If you're thinking about blogging, this platform might be a great place to experiment. Try it for a month. Publish a post once a week, let your contacts know, and see what happens.

Another way to leverage LinkedIn is to start a LinkedIn group on a targeted topic. In the previous chapter, we discussed the importance of participating in a couple of relevant groups. But if you can't find a great group, or if you have an idea for a niche you'd like to discuss with other professionals, start a group to host that conversation. Do some searches on LinkedIn and find people you think might be interested. Invite them to join. It takes a commitment to keep the group active, and you may need to enlist the support of a few friends to participate at first. But if you can get a group going, it puts your name, as the founder and contact person, front and center for every member. And if titled correctly, it could help bring up your name alongside relevant keywords in Google searches.

Start a Blog

Blogging can be an effective way to build authority, and there is much written on the topic of creating a successful blog. Many people blog about personal passions or hobbies. Others focus on some aspect of their profession. This is what we recommend for building authority in your field.

Richard worked with a client in job search whose blog chronicled everything that happened to him (well, nearly everything). You could see him at restaurants and political rallies—even when he spent days in the hospital for back surgery. Richard recommended the client focus for a few weeks on posting information about his passion for his profession and that he should be more careful about posting his personal life. This young man was soon snatched up by the marketplace because he was talented and engaging and articulate about his value. His blog was not necessarily crippling, but it could have been. He's happy he landed in a good role, and as he gets more serious about his career, he's more thoughtful about what type of information he posts publicly.

Now that Mei has had some success as an HR generalist, she has her eye on a management role. She needs to highlight her interest and expertise in supervising others. She likes to write and has a nice, humorous style, so she decides to write a series of blog posts about a topic important to supervision: how to give candid feedback. Mei already has a lot of content on this topic from taking classes and researching.

She realizes the piece doesn't need to be really original—just really helpful. She lets her boss know what she's doing and asks her to review her thinking. She also reaches out to other leaders to ask for stories (good and bad) so she has specific examples to share. When sharing the positive examples, she names names and helps promote those managers. Mei is building key relationships while producing something that associates her with expertise in supervision.

And each time she publishes a blog post, what do you think she does? Yes—she sends an update to her LinkedIn contacts and posts links in relevant LinkedIn groups and on other blogs. It isn't too hard, and she's beginning to make a name for herself.

Publish a Book

Publishing a book is easier than ever. (At least that's what we thought when we stated writing ours.) Today there are better opportunities than ever to publish smaller, more focused books that can be very helpful to a career, particularly for consultants. A published book denotes an air of authority. If the book is well done, then it confers a degree of credibility.

Unless you have a passion for writing and something you feel you must say, don't try to write a masterpiece right out of the chute. If you're writing a book to further your brand and your authority in your professional space, then keep it short and focused. Aim to write a piece that addresses and solves one of your audience's problems. Some people call these "calling card books." They are essentially long how-to articles packaged as books. There's a lot of help out there for doing this, and we outline resources on our website.

Start a Podcast

Another way to get your expertise out there is to create a podcast, or a video podcast if you are comfortable with video as a medium. Podcasts are extremely popular. People follow their favorite thinkers, on the go, on their mobile devices. Before you consider this option, however, listen to some podcasts. Which ones do you really enjoy and find useful? What kind of content can you find for your area of expertise? Listening to podcasts is a great way to stay current in your field. If you like what you find, and you feel you can be a fresh new voice to the discussion, consider podcasting as a part of your own self-promotion strategy. It's like making a radio show every week—some of us think that's really fun!

For a podcast to be successful, it needs to be consistent. As with blogging, you need to produce content on a regular and reliable basis. Every Tuesday morning (or whatever your schedule), you need to release an episode. Pursue this strategy only if you are excited about it, you like the medium, and you have the time.

TAKE ACTION TO POWER YOUR CAREER

You have expertise and plenty to offer, and there's no reason you can't be seen as an expert and thought leader in your field. Just take it a step at a time.

- Pick a specific niche in which you have, or want to develop, expertise. Make sure the subject area is relevant to your audience as well as aligned with your goals.
- Create something—a slideshow, article, blog post, video, presentation. Just pick something and give it a try.
- Once you have generated some valuable content, repurpose it. If you write an article, consider turning the same content into an infographic, a short presentation to deliver at an association meeting, or even a video.

CONCLUSION

I cannot say whether things will get better if we change; what I can say is, they must change if they are to get better.

— G. C. Lichtenberg

What would it feel like to be in charge of your career? To know and be known by people of power and influence? To have recruiters call you with new opportunities? To be invited to join an elite task force? To get the promotion you've been dreaming of? Or simply to be recognized for the contribution you're making to your company and profession? All of this is within reach.

Adopting the mindset and habits of a tactful self-promoter will increase your visibility, unlock opportunities, and ultimately lead to recognition and rewards for the hard work you do.

Adopting the mindset and habits of a tactful self-promoter will increase your visibility, unlock opportunities, and ultimately lead to recognition and rewards for the hard work you do. But nothing will change if you don't change what you're doing. We've made the case that self-promotion is the missing ingredient in many careers, that it is a key career competency, and that it isn't all that difficult or onerous. It just takes a deliberate approach and consistent (but not rigorous) action. You are capable of doing this.

We'll conclude by highlighting some of the ideas that underscore tactful self-promotion, and then we'll have a conversation with our four friends—Mei, George, Natasha, and Henry—who have so generously allowed us to share their stories throughout this book. Having given this self-promotion stuff a try, they have some good insights to share.

But first, here are the key concepts to keep in mind as you start to practice the art of tactful self-promotion.

- **Examine your mindset.** Tactful self-promotion may take you out of your comfort zone, but it still allows you to be authentic.
- **You're in charge of your career.** No one cares more than you do, and no one is as well positioned to take action. You can't expect anyone to help you unless you ask. But if you build strong relationships, you'll have all the help you need!
- **This is doable.** You don't have to do everything in this book. Pick one or two strategies you think are manageable. Try them out. Changing just one thing may well make a big difference in how people view you and recognize your worth.
- **Be authentic.** Yes, that again. Be yourself. (Remember, "Everyone else is already taken.") Find a way to adapt our ideas so they work for you.
- **Prepare for moments.** Be ready for the moments that suddenly present themselves. That is, be prepared to be spontaneous! This requires a little forethought and a sense of mindfulness. Keep an eye on yourself. If you encounter an executive in the elevator, what might you say? What might you say the next time a key leader asks you how things are going? Get in the habit of being prepared.

- **Plan out your own steps.** You don't have to do everything outlined in this book. We've laid out our strategy for tactful self-promotion in a logical sequence: be clear on your positioning, build relationships that matter, and then expand your visibility. However, you don't have to work in that order—start anywhere that makes sense to you. If it's easier to expand your network of acquaintances, start there. If it's easier to write a blog, start there.
- **Build one habit at a time.** Habits don't take effort; building habits does. Establishing a new habit can be hard work, but once you establish that habit, it is simply what you do. It keeps paying off, freeing your energy to focus on other things.
- **Pick a single project to pursue.** In addition to focusing on habits, design a project that supports your longer-term goals and integrates several actions into a single initiative. For example, writing an article (researching a topic, interviewing key people, posting the article on LinkedIn, sending updates to your network) is an integrated project with far greater impact than random actions. One project is easier to implement than a slew of smaller tasks, and projects can often be integrated with your core work activities.
- **Keep learning.** Visit our website, www.TactfulSelfPromotion.com, to discover numerous resources to support your career. Pick a blog to follow or a chapter in the book to reread. Approach this learning as a habit. Just a few minutes a day is all it will take to make a difference.
- **Take action.** Approach this as an experiment. Investing just four hours a month (yes, that's just an hour a week), can move your career in a new direction. If you think ahead about how you want to approach things, you won't blow it. If something doesn't work, modify it or try something else. The only way to blow it is not to try.

MEI, GEORGE, NATASHA, AND HENRY TELL THEIR STORIES

Because Natasha, George, Henry, and Mei have been so gracious to try out some of our suggestions and let us share their stories, we invited them to meet each other. Over dinner and wine, we and our four friends discussed their experiences and learnings. It didn't take much effort to get them talking. Nancy led off the discussion.

Nancy: I feel I know you all so well, and I'm shocked you haven't met yet! Having followed your stories, it seems like each of you has made a great deal of progress. And it seems you were able to do so without being obnoxious or braggy. But you've all definitely strengthened your career prospects.

Richard: We'd love to hear about what you learned about taking charge of your reputations through the art of tactful self-promotion. Who would like to start off?

Mei: I'll go! I don't know about the rest of you, but when I had just finished school and had never worked in a professional job—never even had an internship—I knew *none* of this stuff. I'm just glad I learned about some of these ideas so early in my career and then ran into the people from Acme Industries, who got me thinking about the things I needed to do. I don't know where I would have gone to learn this stuff!

George: Don't be embarrassed that you didn't know a lot about this, Mei. I've been in the business world for more than thirty years and have been pretty successful in my company, and I didn't know some of this either. I can't imagine where I'd be if I had tried out some of these ideas earlier in my career. Staying in just one company, part of my success was due to the fact that everyone knew me and knew that I did good work. Now that I'm on my own, I found that *doing* good work is not the same as *getting* good work. I have to let other people know my value, and this is something I really had to work at. I've tried a few things and am getting better at it, and it's beginning to feel like me.

Henry: Talk about being clueless! I'm an introvert and a technology guy. People in IT don't do any of this—I thought all I needed to do to be successful was get better at writing code and managing software! That's what I thought was the most important thing to move up in my career. Having to look for another job has really taught me a lot. I'm starting to get interviews. I found out there are ways that even introverts can get comfortable talking about themselves. I think I'll be much more successful in the IT world by developing my interpersonal skills—I might even stand out. And perhaps more importantly, I'm learning that I really do enjoy being with other people. And now, after our dinner, I can add four more people to my network. You'll all be getting invitations to link with me on LinkedIn!

Natasha: And I'll be happy to link with you, Henry! Well, I have to say it was a shock to learn that I didn't have enough executive support to get the promotion I wanted. I thought I had been pretty good at managing my career. I had been aware of many things I needed to do in my career, had built up a pretty good network, hired and developed good people, and had great success in product marketing. But it turns out I had not managed up as well as I could have. I've done a few things now that have gained me more visibility, and my boss is telling me that he's hearing good things from his boss and his peers, so I'm making good progress.

George: I found that once I started looking at my network, I had a good number of people that I knew. What I needed to do was articulate my value to others. I found section 1—particularly chapters 2 and 3—to be especially helpful to me. Once I started being able to describe what I can do for people in language they "get" and remember, I started to get some leads. In fact, I can't stay late tonight because I have a second meeting with a potential client tomorrow morning. It feels different being able to describe my value in a way that is comfortable for me but still gets my value across! I'm optimistic that this new business may actually work!

Mei: The most helpful part for me was learning to network. I had never thought about getting organized and getting to know more people who can help me. And I didn't realize how I could help other people—by introducing them to others or sharing resources. Realizing that I can help others made it much easier to approach other people. I got a lot out of Martha's story about changing her mindset.

Henry: That helped me get on the right track too. What helped me most was taking some of the ideas and changing them to fit my style. Some of the things I read that other people had said and done actually turned my stomach. I keep things pretty low-key. However, by taking an idea and modifying it, I made it work for me. I even attended some large meetings, where I reached out to some new people and had a few questions ready to get the conversation going. These questions work like a charm, and this has helped me make more connections that I am confident are going to lead to a job. They already have helped me land a contract assignment.

George: I hear you. I had to modify a few things too to be able to say things in a way that felt natural. And I agree—learning to ask questions that get others to talk is pretty easy, and people like to talk about themselves and their interests. It sort of takes the pressure off of me. Marketing your business is really just about talking and building relationships!

Natasha: Making conversation has never been difficult for me. However, I had to find some strategic ways to get in front of senior people. Once I thought of a good reason—writing an article that they saw as important—it became more natural. In the course of my conversations, I found out some information about their personal interests and their families. So now whenever I see them, I have a host of business and personal topics I am ready to chat about. And I'm getting more comfortable striking up a conversation with any other executive—or people at any level. Thinking ahead and being better prepared has certainly helped me break an important barrier.

Richard: I love hearing how some of these ideas have helped real people tackle some common career issues. I'd like to propose a toast: To some delightful people who took a chance, tried out some of our ideas, and helped us show our readers how it can work. We couldn't have done this book without you! To all of you!

Natasha, George, Henry, Mei: Hear, hear!

Nancy: We'd like to thank all four of you for joining us and sharing your insights. You've inspired us, and we know you've inspired our readers to take action. More wine, anyone?

THE LAST WORD

The core competence of tactful self-promotion is an *art*—it is knowing yourself, understanding situations and cultures, and doing what fits for you. Natasha, George, Henry, and Mei have done a good job illustrating the idea of tactful self-promotion and also have shown us that these ideas really work. They took concepts that were priorities for them and worked on them in their own ways, with good results.

We've laid out a variety of strategies and ideas—now you have to craft your own strategy. We hope you've found the ideas practical and doable. We hope you have a sense of confidence that you can do these things—because you can!—and are not overwhelmed by the number of new ideas. You don't have to do everything, but you must do *something.*

This is an exciting time to be building a career. Things are changing all the time, and we all need to keep learning and adapting to be successful. We wish you the best of luck as you practice the art of tactful self-promotion!

RESOURCES

GENERAL INFORMATION

Careerealism.com

Based on the belief that "every job is temporary," Career Realism is a resource for trusted advice on handling career challenges.

Get Noticed . . . Get Referrals: Build Your Client Base and Your Business by Making a Name for Yourself, by Jill Lublin (McGraw Hill, 2008)

A guide for using powerful self-promotion techniques to get noticed by potential new clients. Lublin focuses on skills required to make a memorable first impression and deepen relationships.

How to Self-Promote without Being a Jerk, by Bruce Kasanoff (Now Possible, 2014)

This book offers quick and effective tips on appropriate self-promotion, structured around a single sentence the author uses to organize his life and his work: "Be generous and expert, trustworthy and clear, open-minded and adaptable, persistent and present."

Inc.com

This site has numerous timely articles about careers, organizations, and business in general.

JibberJobber.com

This tool has evolved into a "personal relationship manager" that allows you to optimize your network relationships as well as manage a job search.

Lean In: Women, Work and the Will to Lead, Sheryl Sandberg (Alfred A. Knopf, 2013)

Sandberg outlines some of the challenges facing women in the workforce and offers suggestions for being leaders at work.

themuse.com

This site has valuable articles about any question you might have about your career, and you can sign up for their free daily newsletter, *The Daily Muse*.

Promote Yourself: The New Rules for Career Success, by Dan Schawbel (St. Martin's Press, 2013)

Schawbel provides a comprehensive approach to building a brand, whether you are managing your career in a company or pursuing an entrepreneurial path.

Quiet Influence: The Introvert's Guide to Making a Difference, by Jennifer B. Kahnweiler, PhD (Berrett-Koehler, 2013)

Kahnweiler encourages introverts to stop trying to act like extroverts, and she offers practical advice for how to leverage the strength of those who want to be quiet influencers. She includes a link to take a Quiet Influence Quotient Self-Assessment.

Quiet: The Power of Introverts in a World that Can't Stop Talking, by Susan Cain (Crown, 2012)

Cain shows how introverts are undervalued and how much the world loses because of this. She introduces us to successful introverts and offers advice on how to better manage in an extroverted world.

Self-Promotion for Introverts: The Quiet Guide to Getting Ahead, by Nancy Ancowitz (McGraw Hill, 2010)

Ancowitz helps introverts tap into their strengths, articulate their accomplishments, and develop strategies for career advancement.

TactfulSelfPromotion.com

Our website contains ideas, tips, tools, and a self-assessment that will help you go beyond the content of this book.

TED.com

This site houses thousands of provocative videos featuring thought leaders in numerous fields, including every aspect of career planning.

What Color Is Your Parachute? 2016: A Practical Manual for Job-Hunters and Career-Changers, Richard N. Bolles (Ten Speed Press, 2015)

This is a classic for a reason—updated every year, it features the latest studies and perspectives on today's job market, including proven strategies for finding jobs even when everyone tells you there are none. It covers everything from cover letters and resumes to networking, interviewing, and negotiating.

Work Reimagined: Uncover Your Calling, Richard J. Leider and David Shapiro (Berrett-Koehler Publishers, 2015)

The world has changed, and so have our options—we all have more opportunities than ever before, if we only had a vision for what we want to do. This book will help clarify your purpose and identify your "calling," so you can start doing the work you were born to do.

POSITION YOURSELF

Career Distinction: Stand Out by Building Your Brand, by William Arruda and Kirsten Dixson (John Wiley & Sons, 2007)

This foundational book by the foremost experts on personal branding provides a blueprint for assessing and expressing your personal brand. Purchase of the book includes access to a Personal Brand Assessment.

The Charisma Myth: How Anyone Can Master the Art and Science of Personal Magnetism, by Olivia Fox Cabane (Penguin, 2012)

Cabane's premise is that charisma is a skill you can learn and practice. She includes practical exercises to help everyone attain presence, power, and warmth.

Ditch, Dare, Do: 3D Personal Branding for Executives, by William Arruda and Deb Dib (Trades Mark Press, 2013)

This quick read provides a plan for defining, aligning, and living the power of brand—with an action plan that can be executed in nine minutes a day!

Growing Your Business! What You Need to Know, What You Need to Do, by Mark LeBlanc (Expert, 2003)

Mark provides many tools and insights, including a model for positioning yourself effectively, in this quick guide for drafting a compelling branding statement.

Power: Why Some People Have It—and Others Don't, by Jeffrey Pfeffer (HarperCollins, 2010)

This Stanford professor talks about the key personal qualities that lead to power and influence.

"Your Body Language Shapes Who You Are," Amy Cuddy, TED Talk, June 2012. (Video and transcript available at www.ted.com/talks/amy_cuddy_your_body_language_shapes_who_you_are?)

A social psychologist who does research on body language provides a simple and motivating approach to increasing your power.

DEVELOP STRATEGIC RELATIONSHIPS

Dig Your Well Before You're Thirsty, by Harvey Mackay (Currency Doubleday, 1990).

A consummate networker, Mackay shares compelling stories and provides actionable advice about how to build and maintain a network of trusted, valuable contacts.

How to Win Friends and Influence People, by Dale Carnegie (Simon & Schuster, 1936)

This timeless classic is as relevant today as when it was written, providing valuable counsel on building self-confidence and listening skills and cultivating authentic human relationships to increase your power and influence.

I'm at a Networking Event: Now What???, by Sandy Jones-Kaminski (HappyAbout, 2009)

A short, practical guide, broken down into tips for preparing for, attending, and following up after attending an event. Lots of links and websites for further information.

Never Eat Alone: And Other Secrets to Success, One Relationship at a Time, by Keith Ferrazzi with Tahl Raz (Currency Doubleday, 2005)

In this connected age, Ferrazzi talks about developing both your mindset and your skillset to connect with colleagues, friends, and associates.

The 20 Minute Networking Meeting: Learn to Network. Get a Job., by Marcia Ballinger, PhD, and Nathan Perez (Keystone Search, 2012)

A short, practical, and straightforward volume of networking advice from a respected search professional. Helps people avoid classic mistakes in building networks.

INCREASE YOUR VISIBILITY

Brag! The Art of Tooting Your Own Horn without Blowing It, by Peggy Klaus (Business Plus, 2003).

This book makes a compelling case for why appropriate self-promotion is essential for recognition and job security.

Business Model You: A One-Page Method For Reinventing Your Career, by Tim Clark and Alexander Osterwalder (Wiley, 2012)

This engaging book offers a visual way to summarize and creatively brainstorm a personal career plan on a single sheet of paper.

Job Searching with Social Media for Dummies, by Joshua Waldman (John Wiley & Sons, 2013)

Although focused on job search, this book offers comprehensive strategies and detailed tactics for using social media to establish relationships and increase visibility with influencers.

LinkedIn.com

The premier website for connecting with other people, staying current in your field, and promoting your own work and brand.

Platform: Get Noticed in a Noisy World, by Michael Hyatt (Thomas Nelson, 2012)

This resource makes a strong case for leveraging social media to promote your own brand and offers practical advice for setting up an integrated platform to promote your brand online.

The Power Formula for LinkedIn Success: Kick-start Your Business, Brand, and Job Search, by Wayne Breitbarth (Greenleaf Book Group Press, 2013)

This best-selling book about LinkedIn covers relevant information in an easy-to-understand format. Wayne's blog is also a terrific resource for keeping up to date with changes and new ideas for leveraging this powerful platform.

ACKNOWLEDGMENTS

So many people have helped us get our ideas from our heads to this book, and we want to thank them.

We have learned so much from our clients, and we want to thank all of those we've worked with over the years for continuing to inspire and teach us. We hope you received as much from us as we did from you. We especially want to thank those whose stories were included in the book.

To our coworkers at Lee Hecht Harrison, especially Dave Reed, an inspiration and mentor, we appreciate the collegiality.

There were a number of readers who gave us thoughtful comments that helped shape the book, including Mary Anderson, Jim Bolton, Anne Burke, Christine Carnicom, Margie Dirks, Carol Kaemmerer, John Leeper, Christine Moore, Cindy O'Schaughnessy, Marg Penn, Susan Reinhart, Julie Scheidler, Dennie Scott, and Dan Verdick.

And thanks to these mentors and supporters without whom this book could never have been born: Sharon Bray, Laura Caccia, Jim Cadena, David Dodson, John Dodson, Sue Dodson, Tim Dunkin, Caela Farren, Tom Karl, Sallie Lillienthal, and Donald Summers.

Matt Gartland of WinningEdits did the first read-through and edit, and his direct but encouraging feedback was invaluable.

To the team at Beaver's Pond Press, we could not have finished this without you! Special thanks to Alicia Ester, Kellie Hultgren, Dan Pitts, and Angie Wiechmann.

A special thanks to Martha for allowing us to use her story. And, of course, to Natasha, George, Henry, and Mei for cooperating and trying out new behaviors to help us illustrate some of our points.

To our families, deep and sincere thanks to Gabrielle and Jim, and our wonderful daughters, Anne, Elizabeth, Melina, and Sofia.

ONE LAST THING...

Please visit our website to tap into resources that will help power your career.

We'd love to hear your stories as well.

www.TactfulSelfPromotion.com

And if you liked the book and want to share your enthusiasm with others, recommend it to friends, post about it on social media, or please write a review on Amazon or Goodreads.